Praise for *Ju*

"*I challenge anyone to read this book and not be powerfully and blissfully changed by it! Lisa is a sparkling example of what she teaches. She excels at the art of being 'happy for no reason.' When you read* **Juicy Joy**, *you'll ride the joyful wave to experiencing self-love, authenticity and fulfillment.*"

— **Marci Shimoff**, *New York Times* best-selling
author of *Happy for No Reason* and *Love for No Reason*

"*Lisa McCourt has developed a brilliant step-by-step system for relocating yourself as the juicy, delicious, vibrant creature you were born to be. Allow these seven steps to launch you into unprecedented heights of self-adoration.*"

— **Regena Thomashauer**, author of
Mama Gena's School of Womanly Arts

"*I love this book! It's honest, from the heart, inspiring, and, like the title says, juicy. Lisa McCourt captures all the values I hold dear and expresses them in a believable, engaging, and exciting way. I hope lots of people will read this and light their soul.*"

— **Alan Cohen**, author of *Enough Already:
The Power of Radical Contentment*

"*Throughout our lives we're faced with challenges to maintaining a positive and joyful outlook on life, and now we finally have a guidebook to turn to. Lisa McCourt has produced a simple yet profound manual for creating a happy and joyful life no matter what your circumstances. She shares vignettes from her personal struggles that readers can readily identify with and details in clear and straight-forward language how you can empower yourself and fill your life with juicy joy. This book can change your life!*"

— **Dr. Steven Farmer**, author of *Earth Magic,
Earth Magic Oracle Cards,* and *Animal Spirit Guides*

Juicy Joy

ALSO BY LISA McCOURT

Books for Adults and Teens

101 Ways to Raise a Happy Baby
101 Ways to Raise a Happy Toddler
Attitude: Tips to Help You Deal, Feel, and Be Real

Children's Books

Chicken Soup for the Soul Reader: Best Night
Chicken Soup for Little Souls: The Best Night Out With Dad
Chicken Soup for Little Souls: The Braids Girl
Chicken Soup for Little Souls: Della Splatnuk, Birthday Girl
Chicken Soup for Little Souls: A Dog of My Own
Chicken Soup for Little Souls: The Goodness Gorillas
Chicken Soup for Little Souls: The Never-Forgotten Doll
Chicken Soup for Little Souls: The New Kid and the Cookie Thief
Good Night, Princess Pruney Toes
Granny's Dragon
Happy Halloween, Stinky Face
I Love You, Stinky Face
I Miss You, Stinky Face
It's the Hundredth Day, Stinky Face
It's Time for School, Stinky Face
Love You Until . . .
Merry Christmas, Stinky Face
The Most Thankful Thing
Time for Kindergarten, Stinky Face
Yummiest Love
. . . and other children's titles

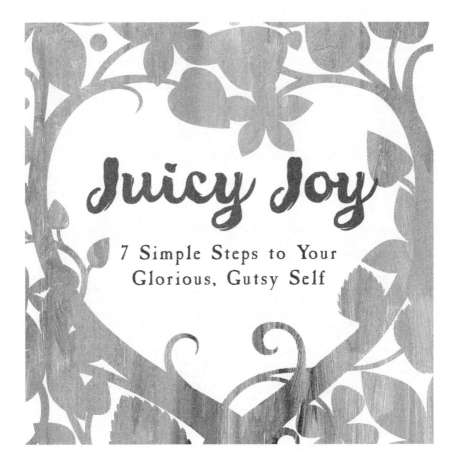

Juicy Joy

7 Simple Steps to Your Glorious, Gutsy Self

LISA McCOURT

HAY HOUSE, INC.
Carlsbad, California • New York City
London • Sydney • Johannesburg
Vancouver • Hong Kong • New Delhi

Published and distributed in the United States by: Hay House, Inc.: www
.hayhouse.com® • **Published and distributed in Australia by:** Hay House
Australia Pty. Ltd.: www.hayhouse.com.au • **Published and distributed in
the United Kingdom by:** Hay House UK, Ltd.: www.hayhouse.co.uk • **Published and distributed in the Republic of South Africa by:** Hay House SA
(Pty), Ltd.: www.hayhouse.co.za • **Distributed in Canada by:** Raincoast:
www.raincoast.com • **Published in India by:** Hay House Publishers India:
www.hayhouse.co.in

Cover design: Julie Davison • *Interior design:* Riann Bender

"The Invitation," by Oriah (**www.oriah.org**) is reprinted by permission. Taken
from the book *The Invitation* © 1999. Published by HarperONE, San Francisco,
CA. All rights reserved.

"The Voice You Hear When You Read Silently" by Thomas Lux is reprinted by
permission. Taken from the book *New and Selected Poems 1975–1999*. Published by
Houghton Mifflin, New York, NY.

The author of this book does not dispense medical advice or prescribe the
use of any technique as a form of treatment for physical, emotional, or medical problems without the advice of a physician, either directly or indirectly. The
intent of the author is only to offer information of a general nature to help you
in your quest for emotional and spiritual well-being. In the event you use any of
the information in this book for yourself, which is your constitutional right, the
author and the publisher assume no responsibility for your actions.

Library of Congress Cataloging-in-Publication Data

McCourt, Lisa.
  Juicy joy : 7 simple steps to your glorious, gusty self / Lisa McCourt.
    p. cm.
  ISBN 978-1-4019-3363-0 (pbk.)
  1. Self-esteem. 2. Self-actualization (Psychology) I. Title.
  BJ1533.S3M35 2012
  158.1--dc23
                                    2011050755

ISBN: 978-1-4019-3363-0
Digital ISBN: 978-1-4019-3364-7

15 14 13 12   4 3 2 1
1st edition, March 2012

*For Lily Kate, Tucker, and Greg. And for every soul
brave enough to honor the deeply buried voice
that whispers its tender longing for more . . .*

CONTENTS

FOREWORD

Lisa McCourt is a daring and adventurous life pioneer. She has spent years reading and studying with the world's greatest personal-growth teachers and applying the wisdom she has gleaned to her own life and that of her fortunate students. It is with much enthusiasm that I introduce you to her genuinely useful book on a very important subject: how to create and nurture a juicy, joyful, fabulous life.

In these pages you will learn dozens of masterful techniques for discovering and accepting your true nature, healing your soul, overcoming your victim story and other obstacles, falling in love with yourself (a prerequisite to having Big Love in your life), and so much more.

As your new BFF, Lisa will take you by the hand and gently guide you, step-by-step, to becoming your highest, juiciest, and best version of yourself.

Lisa knows that she came into this life with a soul plan—to learn and teach ever-evolving levels of transparency and self-love. With great humor and humility, she bravely reveals her own personal life struggles and the unique processes she used to access and begin living as her most juicy, joyful self.

Unlike many who teach the value of positive thinking, Lisa wisely makes space for acknowledging and feeling our negative

emotions. As she rightly asserts, "You're human, and stuff is going to piss you off." She teaches a brilliant process called Emotion-Mixing and explains that by knowing and finding the gift in all of our emotions, we learn from them, leading to greater joy, love, and expansion. Oh, how I wish I had read this book 25 years ago—the money and time I could have saved myself!

One of the things about life that I know for sure is this: We are powerful beings who have the ability to co-create our life with the Universe. We can change our minds, our thoughts, our emotions, and the events of our life when we choose to apply our time, energy, intention, and attention. If you are ready and willing to follow each of the 7 Steps to Your Glorious, Gutsy Self outlined in this book, I promise you will be forever and fabulously changed by it.

With love,
Arielle Ford

~C C~

PREFACE

The Juicy Joy Story

A garlic-infused breeze kicks up the palm fronds beside the table at my favorite neighborhood bistro. "What do you want?" Sarah asks me. Her kids and my kids—all smart, sweet, and beautiful—chase one another around the plaza fountain. Sarah gets up to bring them wishing coins.

What do I want?

I want more.

I want to crash out of this invisible armor I'm trapped in—to tear away the shackles and freefall, delirious and wild. I want uninhibited, unbridled, uncontained passion. I want to plummet naked into a velvet ocean at midnight and roll in the ecstasy of the waves.

I want to peel back my layers and hold my raw wounds up to the sun for healing.

I want to slice through these suffocating wrappings and grab onto <u>core me</u>—whoever that is—and never let her go; make her into the real me, the only me, for some to love and some not to love . . . and I want to not so painfully care who does and who doesn't.

I want to feel, taste, devour it all—no filters, no censors, no gate-keeper telling me what is rightfully mine to take and what isn't. I want rapture. I want free, primal abandon at the top of a mountain under a full moon. I want to absorb me, embrace me, the light and the dark, the glorious and the hideous, and cherish it all and laugh at it all forever.

Sarah's back. "So what do you want?" she asks.

What do I want? "Caprese salad and a cup of pasta fagioli."

We close our menus and clink our chiantis as my daughter slides, sweaty and precious, into my lap.

I eventually did tell my friend what I wanted—after many years of clawing away at truths I had never before allowed myself to glimpse. Truths that tugged at me like a feverish itch, just under the skin, so close and ever present, yet so ephemeral, so elusive when I chased them. This book represents my journey, but it's a guide to accessing your *own* Juicy Joy. A direct, streamlined path you can follow, in case you're wanting free of your armor, too. Come with me. We'll start right here and end up on that mountaintop. You in?

Answer thoughtfully. Juicy Joy is not for the faint of heart, the meek, or anyone who feels destined for only a good-enough life. Juicy Joy is for you if you're ready to take on more—more substance, more bliss, more willingness to experience the full spectrum of a rich, multilayered existence.

Living in Juicy Joy is the opposite of living numb. It's bold, exciting, and completely attainable no matter how far you might feel you are from it at the moment. My path to Juicy Joy was long and circuitous, but yours is neatly mapped out for you, and you're already holding it in your hands.

How Juicy Joy Was Born

I am the poster child for the popular Richard Bach quote, "We teach what we need to learn." At age 14, I read Wayne Dyer's *Your Erroneous Zones,* taking copious notes and copying passages from it into my journal. I'm sure the title's wordplay was lost on me, but the book's message wasn't. From that moment on, I was hooked. In college I was so fascinated with comparative religion that a maverick psychology professor allowed me to create a credited independent study program on the overlap between modern metaphysics and ancient spiritual thought.

I went on to devour every pop-psychology and metaphysical book or training I could find, taking dozens of the most notable courses and working with some of the world's top coaches and gurus. What I appreciated most about all of these experiences was how remarkably similar they were, and how their principles almost always were based in the ancient truths I'd learned from my comparative religion studies. When I discovered the spirit family of Abraham, presented by Esther and Jerry Hicks, I was thrilled to have found such a comprehensive and contemporary source of these same ancient truths, and I became an avid student of Abraham's wisdom.

My lifelong passion for personal development seemed to be serving me well. It was good stuff, and I was a diligent pupil. Early on, I became a powerful manifester who created an adult life that was, by all objective measures, fantastic. I had a wonderful, supportive husband; two sweet, smart kids; a beautiful home in my favorite part of the country; stellar health; time for volunteer work; plenty of friends; and a successful, dream career as a speaker and author of parenting books and children's titles that were selling millions of copies.

And I was always the cheerful one. Everywhere I went, people commented on my smile, my agreeable nature. I always looked the part—to anyone who might be forming any opinion of me, anywhere. The right suburban car, the right clothes, the right social life, the great kids in the great schools, brought up by the best parenting principles.

It's not like I even consciously felt the lie. I told myself everything was perfect all the time. It had to be. Perfect, perfect, all the time. What would happen if I stopped being perfect for a second? Devastation. If I stopped being perfect, who would love me?

And without perpetual love from everyone around me, how would I survive?

It sounds ridiculous, but that was the core belief I uncovered. If I stopped smiling, if I stopped pleasing, if I stopped doing the dance everyone enjoyed me doing because it made their lives easier, or lighter, or whatever—if I stopped any of that for even a second, the love-well would surely run dry, and I'd shrivel up into a hard, cold ball of ash and disintegrate into nothing. So I couldn't stop. Ever.

And if I started to feel empty and vacuous and lifeless inside, as long as I kept playing all the right parts on the outside, I'd be okay. Maybe with the right affirmations, or with the next self-help book, or the next seminar, I'd be able to patch that up without anyone ever being the wiser. And if I couldn't patch it up, at least I was always really, really good at hiding it, and as long as it stayed hidden, everything would be fine.

I woke up one day to the regrettable realization that despite all of the personal work I'd done, there was a substantial layer I'd yet to crack. I'd accumulated a wealth of supremely valuable knowledge, but I'd only been applying it to half of me—the half I could bear to own, the identity I'd so painstakingly crafted. I'd been unwittingly plastering layer upon layer of spiritual platitudes over a damaged and wounded core that I had never dared acknowledge, much less dive fearlessly into.

Out of that critical awareness, Juicy Joy was born. With laser-like clarity, I suddenly knew that authenticity and self-love were the keys to the kingdom. Without them, nothing else can bring you joy. With them, nothing can *fail* to bring you joy.

How Juicy Joy Was Spread

In the late 1990s, when I started getting invitations to speak at schools across the country as a best-selling author of children's books, I talked about my books and about writing. But that didn't seem fair. The whole student body was required to attend, and

evening presentations were often requested for the school staff and parents. It seemed to me that all those hundreds of people couldn't possibly be interested in writing, so I switched the focus of my presentations to "creativity."

Since I was such a spirituality and self-dev junkie, it didn't take long for me to start taking liberties with the word *create*. I'd gloss over the requisite blah-blah-blah about creating art, literature, poetry, and so on. Then I'd launch, with relish, into what I loved best—teaching these adults and kids how to "create" situations and outcomes, how to create themselves, and how to be masterful creators of their own lives.

I was afraid the national school system would catch on to my bait-and-switch tactics and stop inviting me, but the opposite happened! Word of mouth about my unconventional approach to teaching creativity got me more school bookings than I could handle. The evening presentation to the adults became the biggest selling point of my visits. Eventually, the school visits led into all kinds of adult speaking gigs at national writers' conferences and spirituality conferences. I started leading workshops at libraries, spiritual centers, and stores.

During my first decade as an author, I'd felt a calling to help children grow up feeling unconditionally lovable and unquestionably valuable as their true, unique selves. All my training had pointed to the irrefutable conclusion that self-love was the ticket to healthy emotional development, so I'd felt compelled to bump up the worldwide average on the number of kids who are brought up feeling unconditionally loved. After selling more than five and a half million books to parents and children, that goal felt satiated, and I was ready to move on to a new passion: helping millions of *adults* feel that same kind of intrinsic, sublime worth and self-honoring, even if it meant feeling it for the first time.

I was thrilled to have so many opportunities to share my love of New Thought material with mainstream-thinking audiences, and even more thrilled by their apparent appreciation for my unique delivery and personal perspectives on these ancient principles. I became an enthusiastic New Thought broker. My early presentations consisted mostly of me telling my audiences about the most recent fascinating modalities I'd tried and reviewing the powerful books I'd read, always through the filter of how each concept could help one become more authentic and self-loving.

It was exhilarating to realize that I was opening up magical and promising new worlds for people! My passion for this kind of "recruiting" eventually overshadowed my other professional passions, and I began shaping my plethora of adult-workshop materials into the book you are now reading. I knew I'd hit upon a system for never having to settle, ever, when it came to the amount of joy and richness I experienced in my life. And I couldn't think of any greater life purpose than to help others discover that same secret.

If you want to learn the easiest, most effective ways to step into your own true greatness and love the hell out of your precious self, come hang with me. I will set you up.

INTRODUCTION

What Do You Want?

I'll be up-front with you; I'm hoping to suck you in. I have accomplished a miraculous life transformation through the application of 7 steps that have proven to be appealing and powerful, not only to New Thought enthusiasts, but to the utterly uninitiated as well.

Maybe you're somewhere in between—just on the cusp of discovering the life-altering benefits of personal development. You might be one of the millions of those "cuspers" who are desperate for answers but don't know where to turn. Maybe you wouldn't be caught dead in a metaphysical bookstore or let yourself be spotted in "that aisle" of Barnes & Noble. But even if you scoff at the blatantly hippy-dippy, you've surely notice all the recent buzz about creating reality with your thoughts and the magical ability some people have to attract amazing circumstances. Maybe you're curious but still somewhat reluctant to own your curiosity. If so, this book is for you. It's for you simply because you've realized you want more *life* out of your life—want to *feel* more, *experience* more, and break out of your rut.

Juicy Joy's 7 steps will get you there. You'll first get clear about who you are—not just who you routinely consider yourself to be, the person you habitually show the world, but who you are in the deepest recesses of your authentic heart and soul. Once you've brought the truest you out into the light, you'll learn how to fall so madly in love with that glorious creature that you never feel the need to hide it again. You'll feel blissfully comfortable in your own skin. And from that vantage point, in the words of Franz Kafka, "the world will freely offer itself to you. . . . It will roll in ecstasy at your feet."

That's what I mean by "juicy." It's called "Juicy Joy" because the level of experience I want for you is so much richer and fuller than the smiley, fluffy kind of happiness we often associate with the word *joy.* Juicy Joy is rooted in extraordinary self-knowledge and self-appreciation. Because here's the big secret. The only reason you don't have everything you want in your life is simple and irrefutable: *You don't love yourself enough to believe you deserve everything you want.*

Read that sentence again. Even if you don't consciously think that's true, it is. The life you have right now is the precise, exact measure of what you subconsciously believe you deserve and how much you love yourself. The secret to elevating every aspect of your life—love, money, health, life purpose, or whatever floats your boat—is simply to elevate your self-love.

But before you can genuinely, deeply love yourself, you have to *know* yourself in a way most of us routinely avoid. That means honestly examining where you stand today, and identifying all the areas in which your outer circumstances are not a match to your core truth—the person you know yourself to be inside. Closing that gap is the route to radical authenticity, the springboard for Juicy Joy.

It's not about shining yourself up or changing or improving yourself. It's just about peeling away the masks that you've accumulated over your true glorious essence. When we become alert to these masks, we can deliberately observe them with curiosity, even with awe and admiration at their strength and cleverness. We can be amused by them. Only then will we fully understand that we are sovereign over our personal energy, and wearing the masks or removing them is entirely our choice.

In Steps One through Four of your Juicy Joy journey, you'll learn the powerful arts of Emotion-Mixing, Filter-Fixing, Judgment-Flipping, and Story-Stripping. These are the deconstructing Steps that will peel away the layers of conditioning that have been camouflaging the real you. We all accumulate these layers just by virtue of growing up in the society we live in. They must be stripped away if we want to make the kinds of valuable discoveries that lead to substantial, permanent shifts.

In Step Five: Taco-Filling, you'll begin the restructuring process with a fresh clarity that will allow you to define your desires with delicious, colorful precision. You'll blast through the subconscious blocks that have been limiting your capacity for juicy, *juicy* abundance—abundance in money, love, respect, freedom . . . wherever you've been feeling a lack. You'll unleash your desires into the Universe with unsurpassed confidence and giddy anticipation of their certain fruition.

Step Six: Gut-Dripping, will shed light on all your relationships and show you how to bring that shiny-new authentic you into meaningful, fulfilling partnership with others. You'll recognize the patterns and unconscious behaviors that have been sabotaging your relationships, and you'll learn what was causing them and how to reverse them. Simple, pleasurable exercises will guarantee that you start attracting and enjoying the kind of love and closeness you've always dreamed of.

You'll deeply anchor your journey and all the scrumptious shifts you've made with the final step, God-Dipping. This step will show you how to relax fully into the loving arms of the Universe that adores you, so that you never have to expend a drop of your precious energy on worry or stress, ever again.

Each step is artfully designed to bring you ever closer to the life you've always known should be yours—the life that's always felt just out of reach. Each premise is explained and illustrated with real-life anecdotes—both mine and those of my students. Time-tested, exceedingly effective exercises allow you to personalize the steps, integrating them one by one into your own life situation.

We are all authentic and self-loving at our cores because our animating source is love itself. It's only our false beliefs and fears that separate us from our authentic, self-loving core beings. Dis-satisfaction is always the result of splits within you. You have all these voices talking to you all the time, and it's uncomfortable to not know which one to listen to.

That's when Juicy Joy becomes a discernment practice. You'll learn to listen carefully, honor each voice, and be grateful for them all. You'll know how to get clear about what each voice is representing and how it got there, so that the *one* voice can easily pop out among them—the voice that is your true self, your higher wisdom, the mainline to source energy.

We all have that voice within us; there are no exceptions. Our other voices are just so noisy, and we don't know how to turn them down. You're about to learn the best techniques and prac-tices for taking care of those different parts of you—loving and appreciating every voice, while gently sorting them so that there's no question about which one to tune in and listen to. Once you start regularly following the guidance of *that* voice, your life will never be the same.

THE JUICE-SEEKER'S GUIDE TO THE UNIVERSE (HOW TO USE THIS BOOK)

Juicy Joy is spiritual, but it's selfish, too. It's all about you. The word *authenticity* is misunderstood sometimes. People think of it as a virtue, like honesty . . . like you owe the world your authenticity and should feel bad if you're not authentic. You won't find that position here. Juicy Joy training isn't a "should" training. I'm not suggesting you *should* become more authentic because it will make you a better person—you already are a phenomenal person.

I'm telling you that becoming more authentic is your golden ticket: to joy, to success, to vibrant health and energy, to easily manifesting the life of your dreams. It's every bit that transformative. You're not doing this to better serve the world; you're doing it to better serve you. But—happy bonus!—it happens to be the best way to serve your loved ones and the world as well.

Only through radical authenticity and self-love is deep, enduring joy possible. The 7 steps in this process are simple, but they're not easy. They're straightforward, but they require personal bravery and determination. They will set you free, but only if you're ready to bask in the sublime release that comes with full emotional freedom.

Know Thyself

Many people dabble halfheartedly with affirmations or positive thinking, only to quit, disappointed, when they don't get the results they desire. But personal-development strategies that lead you away from thorough examination of what is presently most authentic for you are destined to fail, or at best to work only on a superficial level. After all, how can you chart a course to a desired destination without first knowing, with the utmost clarity, precisely where you are?

The only way to meaningfully change your external circumstances is to change your internal circumstances, and that change can only happen from a point of deep and extensive self-knowledge. We're going on a spelunking expedition through your personal catacombs—all those nooks and crannies you've kept carefully sealed off, and some you never even knew were there. Pack your shiniest flashlight and come prepared to get utterly real with the only person who truly matters: you.

Who would you like to be at our journey's end? Only you can decide that, and you have infinite choices available to you. If that assertion sounds like New Agey gobbledygook, I challenge you to revisit your opinion when you've finished this book. If you're craving a shift in any area of your life, you'll find the strength here to make genuine changes wherever you need them. But they'll be from the inside out. It's the only kind of change that works. Outside-in changes are unsatisfying and temporary at best. They don't foster sustainable Juicy Joy.

You're going to shift your circumstances by shifting *you*, and that can only happen when you fully, excruciatingly, *know* you. It's possible that just knowing, finally, who you truly are—just shining a light on every last speck of you—is all that you'll need to open the floodgates to a delicious deluge of Juicy Joy! At the very least, self-awareness will provide an opening through which Juicy Joy will begin to trickle into your life, and there's plenty here to get you to the tidal wave.

We've all clung to situations that sell us short but feel safe, to stories that excuse us from being in our highest joy, to elaborately constructed, illusory representations of our lives, so that we can prove to everyone—including ourselves—that we *are* the facades we choose to project. It's these little white lies, half-truths, and self-deceptions we weave around and through our lives that form the invisible armor that imprisons us.

Being totally honest with yourself about yourself is terrifying! Almost no one routinely does it! Yet that is your goal on this journey. Only through meticulous self-discovery will you reach Juicy Joy. And you will be so happy that you pushed through to this place of rare insight and complete self-adoration because it will touch every aspect of your life in miraculous ways! Your intuition will shine forth unimpeded. Synchronistic opportunities will unfold with uncanny regularity. Your relationships will become blissful, and free-flowing enthusiasm will fuel your days.

Juicy Joy gives you permission to dream loudly. It validates all those niggly little feelings you've been having that you've never allowed yourself to express to anyone, including yourself. Where else can you be rewarded for your petulance? Encouraged to get small-minded? Praised for wallowing in your own petty grievances? Surprising exercises will take you through all of those emotional catacombs you've sealed off over the years. Your best tool for clearing out these emotional catacombs will be NakedWriting.

Let's Get Naked

I call the Juicy Joy writing exercises "NakedWritings." You don't have to actually take off your clothes to do them (that's optional!), but you do have to set a conscious intention to be as emotionally naked and vulnerable as you possibly can, because that's what will yield the best result.

You will need a dedicated Juicy Joy notebook, and you must promise me that you will keep it with this book and have it right next to you, along with a pen, whenever you're reading this. Choose something that's comfortable to work with (I'm a fan of spiral notebooks). No one else need ever see what comes out of your NakedWritings, so don't hold anything back.

Do not think about spelling or grammar; do not think about anyone's opinion about what you're writing. Try not to *think* at all. Stream-of-consciousness gobbledygook is what you're going for. Do not erase or cross out. Just keep going. Force yourself to continuously put marks on the paper—the less forethought you give to each word in a NakedWriting, the better. You want to keep forging ahead without judgment, because you'll often find that your first thoughts are your surface thoughts, and those must be purged out of the way before your true inner voice can be heard.

You'll be doing some list making. You may notice that sometimes I will ask you to make a list similar to one you have already made for an earlier exercise. Resist the temptation to skip it or look back in your journal at the earlier list. Make a new one, with whatever comes up for you. You will be shifting many perspectives as you work through this book. At any point in your journey, you could easily have a very different reaction to a question than the reaction you had at an earlier point.

NakedWritings will often kick off your Juicy Joy transformational processes. The NakedWritings will dig up buried aspects of you so that you can use their results to personalize the next bits of the integration.

Transforming the Energy of Your Beliefs Through JuicyFeels

Where in your life are you on autopilot, creating the same situation for yourself (in essence) over and over again? Maybe you keep dating the same romantic partner. Maybe the current model is better looking, or more successful, or slightly more open than the one before . . . but in essence you're with a lover who triggers your tried-and-true insecurities, defense mechanisms, and familiar unhealthy spirals.

Or maybe you find yourself in the same employment dynamic over and over again—even if you change careers completely. Maybe you've attracted a series of supervisors, or a series of friends, who stir up the not-good-enough feelings a parent invoked for you as a child. In the coming steps, we're going to be looking closely at how these patterns develop and how to benefit from the opportunities they offer.

You'll begin living from a place of higher awareness—with a fresh understanding of how to work with the energy field that connects everything and everyone in the universe. If that tips your bullshit-o-meter, it shouldn't. It's a matter of verifiable science that everything you see, touch, and experience is made up of energy vibrating at different frequencies. We've come to the point in our human evolution where people are learning to use their intuition to work with these frequencies, and it's time for you to get on board. Even Einstein said that "the only truly valuable thing is intuition," and he's the guy who *defined* energy with the whole $E=mc^2$ thing, remember?

Oprah Winfrey is one of the most admired, successful, and wealthy people on the planet. Ever wonder how she got that way? Maybe it's because she understands energy. On her final show, she said, "You are responsible for your life. What is your life? What is all life? What is every flower, every rock, every tree? Energy! And you're responsible for the energy you create for yourself, and you're responsible for the energy that you bring to others. . . . All life is energy, and we are transmitting it every moment. We are beaming it . . . little tiny signals, like radio frequencies, and the world is responding in kind."

Your Juicy Joy practice will focus on the deliberate rewiring of your belief system because *your beliefs are the energy that is determining everything you experience as your reality.* That's not New Age speak anymore; it's common knowledge. It's why researchers always have to use placebo control groups whenever they test any drug. If they don't have a group taking a sugar pill, their findings won't be considered valid by the agencies that govern pharmaceuticals. In pain-control experiments, when a new pain pill is tested, fully half of the sufferers who are given a placebo will report having less pain. The mind is that powerful, and the scientific community knows it. Changing your mind will change your life.

If you aren't living the precisely blissful, richly textured life you crave, you will soon know which of your beliefs are keeping you from it, and you'll know what to do about that. Most of your limiting beliefs are not unique to you; our culture suffers from a long-standing epidemic of crappy shared beliefs.

Most of us, at some level, harbor the same fears, the same tragic self-doubts, and the same profound longings to be liberated from our self-made prisons. In our outer circumstances, we may vary greatly, but at deeper levels, this is seldom the case. The transformational tool you'll be using to rewire your belief system is the always-pleasurable, scientifically substantiated "JuicyFeel."

JuicyFeels Get the Juice Flowing

JuicyFeels are absolutely essential to your journey, so don't ever skip over them or rush through them. They are similar to visualizations, except rather than emphasizing mental sight, JuicyFeels emphasize feeling your emotions and their corresponding bodily sensations.

For many years, I used the word *feelingizations* for these Juicy Joy processes. I had appropriated this term from my beloved friend Arielle Ford, who had brilliantly invented it to make the point that visualizations don't do squat unless you *feel* the thing you're visualizing. I liked it for the additional reason that not all people are visually oriented, and the term *visualization* can be frustrating for those who are not.

JuicyFeels are dressed-up feelingizations with a few added components. A lot of people are living their lives *dry*, and if that describes you, you know what I mean. JuicyFeels get the juice flowing again. People who have dried out are always looking for things outside of themselves to try to get the juice back, but the whole point of this book is that getting the juice pumping *internally* is what will put the juicy stuff in your *external* life.

Once you start doing your JuicyFeels, their components will quickly become second nature to you, but I'll break them down now so you'll understand their origins.

You'll Begin Each JuicyFeel by Moving Pleasurably

I love yoga, but I don't get to classes nearly as often as I'd like. Instead, I have a long-standing habit of moving my body in yoga-like ways that feel good to me while engaged in other activities such as talking on the phone or helping kids with homework. It's kind of like stretching, but with no plan or agenda, and my kids have always loved making fun of it.

A few years ago I was in a workshop called "Self-Discovery Life Mastery," and we were instructed at one point to get up and move and stretch in any way our bodies told us to. I giggled to myself at this legitimizing of what my kids so loved to tease. In the workshop, they called it "intuitive yoga." Of course I was all over that, and ever since then I've proudly defended my importantly labeled activity. Before I had any idea what I was doing, I must have intuitively realized that pleasurably moving my body would automatically release me from mental activity.

Thinking is not the Juicy Joy way. Your thoughts will spin you in endless, frustrated little circles. The only way to get clarity and insight and access your higher wisdom is to pull out of those mental spirals and tune in to your feelings instead.

To start off each JuicyFeel, you'll spend a few moments moving your body in some pleasurable way, focusing all your attention on your bodily sensations. When your attention is focused on your body, you've switched from thinking mode to feeling mode, and that's where you need to be for a JuicyFeel.

You'll Do Your JuicyFeels in Alpha Brain-Wave State

The alpha brain-wave state is already very familiar to you. You're in alpha during that drowsy interlude between being awake and asleep, or whenever you're peacefully daydreaming. Your brain is super receptive to suggestions while in this state, which is why you're always told to relax and breathe deeply when entering into a meditation or hypnosis situation.

Your imagination is able to powerfully influence your subconscious mind when you're in alpha because your subconscious can't tell the difference between a vividly imagined event and reality. Deeply engaging in specific imaginative journeys while in the alpha state will allow you to reprogram long-entrenched beliefs. It's also the most receptive state for hearing the inner voice that connects you to universal wisdom.

I heard on a radio show that Thomas Edison valued the insights he got from this semiconscious state so much that he developed a technique for intentionally mining them. He'd allow himself to get very tired, then sit in a chair so that his hands hung over the edge of the chair's arms. He'd have placed metal pans on the floor beneath each hand, and he'd hold ball bearings over the pans. As he began to fall asleep, his hands would relax, and as soon as he heard the *plink* of the metal on metal, he'd wake up and instantly write down any impressions or thoughts that were going through his mind. Brilliant! And this dude came up with some pretty kickin' ideas.

I'm sure you've heard about the studies done with athletes that have proven that mental rehearsal is nearly as effective as physical rehearsal in terms of improving performance. There is now scads of scientific evidence proving that imagining an action causes the same neurons to fire in your brain as would fire if you were actually doing the thing.

Maybe Albert Einstein had a hunch about the neurons when he said, "Your imagination is your preview of life's coming attractions." Maybe not. But he was right, and alpha is the brain-wave frequency of imagination. Nikos Kazantzakis concurred when he noted, "By believing passionately in something that does not yet exist, we create it. The nonexistent is whatever we have not sufficiently desired."

It's not difficult to intentionally drop into alpha brain-wave frequency. If your mind is especially busy, it will take longer to get to alpha, but the more regularly you do it, the quicker the process will get—and soon you'll be able to drop in almost immediately simply by intending it.

There are numerous ways to reach alpha, so I'm going to give you several that you can practice in preparation for your Juicy-Feels. To begin each of them, take several slow, deep breaths, focusing all your intention on the movement of the air in and out of your body. From there, experiment with each of the following and see what works best for you:

- Close your eyes and mentally scan your entire body, from top to bottom, slowly bathing every muscle in your loving attention as you release and relax it.

- Slowly count backward from 100, picturing each number in your mind's eye.

- Mentally, rhythmically, repeat a mantra or any calming, soothing word such as *peace, love,* or *tranquility.*

- Gaze at a candle or focus on a mental image of a candle or waterfall.

For many years my favorite method for getting into alpha was a Buddhist practice of dropping my energetic focal point down into my heart center and imagining breathing through that space. I've worked with this method long enough that I now experience the dropping down as a very real physical sensation. I can do it anytime, anywhere, and feel its immediate relaxation benefits.

I learned an extension to this practice a few years ago from my extraordinary coach Rachael Jayne Groover, through her feminine leadership program. Rachael taught me to drop that energetic focal point down lower, down into my hip area, just behind and below my belly button. If you've done any qigong, Eastern breathing techniques, or Taoist meditation, you might know this space as your lower *dantian* center or *hara*.

Once I learned to breathe from both the heart center and hara center together, it became my favorite practice for getting into alpha. I don't even save it for meditation or JuicyFeels. Dropping my point of consciousness down to hara during regular life makes me feel centered, powerful, and sexy as hell. I always have a little hip swagger goin' on when I'm there.

None of the above shortcuts to alpha brain-wave frequency are going to completely obliterate your thoughts, but they should slow them down enough for you to notice a discernable shift in your serenity level. Experiment with them and see which works best for you. If none of them make you feel noticeably more quiet and peaceful, you may be someone who will need to mediate before each JuicyFeel.

The JuicyFeels we'll be doing throughout our journey in this book are a form of meditation in themselves, but if you're not a seasoned meditator, I don't want you to freak out about that. There's really nothing to it. Meditation is a different experience for everyone, so do whatever you need to do to make it enjoyable and relaxing for you.

Play around with the following basic meditation for quieting your mind. Try to do it for at least five minutes if you're new to meditation, and longer if you're not:

- Assume any sitting or supine position that's comfortable for you and take a few slow, deep breaths.

- Imagine a magnificent, full tree in the fall. The leaves are all gorgeous colors. Admire them in your imagination and pretend that each leaf represents a thought.

- Acknowledge that some of these thoughts have the potential to trigger negative emotions and some have the potential to trigger positive emotions. Appreciate your fascinating, diverse thoughts, assembled so majestically on this tree.

- Focus on your breathing while holding the image of the tree. As you notice a thought pop up, without judging it in any way, just mentally say, "There's one," and watch one leaf fall off the tree and gently drop to the ground.

- When the next thought pops up, say, "There's another one," and watch that leaf drift down to the ground.

This meditation practice serves several purposes. It trains you to appreciate all your thoughts and emotions as equal contributors to one beautiful mosaic. And it releases you from the common meditator's struggle of battling the thoughts that pop up when you're trying to empty your mind. Keeping your attention on the whole tree will keep you from being as distracted by the individual thoughts. And when you are, inevitably, distracted by one, you'll have a method for observing it without reaction or resistance.

When preparing for your JuicyFeels, you may determine that you need a few moments of meditation to get yourself into alpha brain-wave state, or you may find that the shortcuts work for you. Whatever you decide is just right. You'll know you're in alpha when you feel deeply relaxed and comfortably distanced from your busy mind chatter.

Indulge in the Power of Pretending

Think of your JuicyFeels as indulgent fantasy breaks. You want to reach back in your consciousness to the way you used to pretend as a child. Remember how vividly real your make-believe games would get? Remember how you could feel the excitement and other emotions in your body just by painting such clear scenarios with your imagination?

My kids and I were playing with my three-year-old niece, Isabella, the other day. In the midst of the boisterous game we'd devised, she suddenly stood perfectly still, staring vacantly into space. When my daughter tried to engage her, Isabella brought her finger to her lips with a fervent, "Shh! I'm at the library." We stood obediently silent for a few moments, until Izzy was done at the library and wanted to play with us again. You're about to get *that good* at laser-focused pretending.

The most effective way to experience your JuicyFeels is to download the free audio files at **JuicyJoy.com** so you can close your eyes and just listen. You can keep the files on your phone or portable device and have them handy whenever you need them. These audios have an extra-special added benefit: They're embedded with subliminal messages that work directly on your subconscious programming! Created with Eldon Taylor's patented InnerTalk® technology, these audio JuicyFeels are powerful tools of transformation, so be sure to use them whenever you can.

If you're tech-shy or just don't have access to the web, read each JuicyFeel through to the end, and then go into the imaginary scene from memory. Don't obsess about the clock, but try to stay in each JuicyFeel for a minimum of five minutes, and much longer if you can.

Some of your JuicyFeels are meant to be done every day. Do them *several times* a day if you'd like. The more time you can spend with them, the faster and more dramatically you'll see their results. We'll be *adding* to some of your most important JuicyFeels as we go along. They should always feel wonderful to you; after all, JuicyFeels are powerful emotional journeys that, done regularly, will dramatically alter your life.

Once you're comfortable in a JuicyFeel, see if there's any kind of a smell you can associate with something in this imaginary scene. It could make sense, or not. It's okay if it's totally incongruent, because any combination that's out of the ordinary and kind of shocking makes a deeper impression on the subconscious, and therefore works even better for our purposes. It could be your baby's head, your grandma's homemade lasagna, some pine trees, or your favorite bubble bath or candle smell. Don't force this step, and don't sweat it if it doesn't feel right. But look for opportunities to incorporate smell whenever you can, because it provides a nearly magical way to reenter your JuicyFeel at will.

Occasionally, a JuicyFeel will ask you to imagine yourself doing some sort of movement while deeply immersed in a certain feeling. This technique "sets" the feeling into your energetic body-mind so that later repeating the movement will give rise to the feeling. Your mind is located in every cell of your being, not just up in your brain like you've been led to believe. That's why cloning is possible, why people can tell things about you from your handwriting, and how martial arts experts are able to break boards in their karate practice by believing that they can. Combining an intentional feeling with a corresponding body movement will help you more deeply incorporate and access the new feeling you want to ingrain.

Don't Pussyfoot Toward Your Juicy Joy— Hurl Yourself Recklessly Aboard!

NakedWritings and JuicyFeels will absolutely transform your world. Maybe that's hard for you to believe at this moment. If so, I urge you to do them anyway. *Especially* if it's hard for you to believe! What have you got to lose? If it doesn't work, you're right where you started. If it does (and it will), you will have discovered pure gold—a pleasurable, free, easy way to have everything you've ever wanted.

Your Juicy Joy training will give you the ability to witness yourself while you do your life. It makes every moment sweet. It's like you're watching a movie about a character you deeply love. You're rooting for this character, even as he gets into difficult scrapes and has his heart broken. You understand what a lovable, remarkable character this is, so you know he's going to pull through. You feel his tragedies with him, but always with the clear expectation that things are about to turn wonderful.

Almost none of the core principles you're about to learn originated with me. They're the principles I read about and encountered again and again in the courses and workshops I've taken, and before that they were the big ideas I devoured in college when I was obsessed with ancient religions and philosophies, most notably Indian Vedic and Buddhist wisdom. The tenets of those two religions, together with the more recent teachings of Abraham, provide the foundation for Juicy Joy. As I built upon that foundation, I was influenced by many treasured teachers you'll find listed in the resource section at the back of this book.

I adore the teachers I've had in this field. I don't just mean that I'm grateful to them, or that I have respect and admiration for them. I deeply love these people—many of whom I've never met, and many of whom lived centuries ago. They've saved my life. It's every bit that dramatic. They're the reason I wanted to join this team.

I created the steps you're about to take by meditating on the combined wisdom I'd gained from all these masters and allowing the cream to rise. I knew which precise nuggets were most profoundly responsible for my own transformation to authenticity and self-love, and I knew I'd been given my journey so that I could grow these nuggets, shaping and synthesizing them into the most powerfully effective process possible for leading you to achieve similar transformation.

Each of the 7 steps to your glorious, gutsy self has its own chapter, and each will take you deeper into an appreciation for your core being and your infinite power. Every new step builds upon the one before it. Many of the practices you'll be doing were born out of my experiences with similar exercises I'd come across frequently in my journey. By combining my own insights with the most potent, most valuable aspects of these popular, classically proven processes, I've supercharged their power to get you the most dramatic, speedy results.

Having spent countless hours both in personal-development workshops and reading pop-psych, metaphysical, and self-dev books, I can honestly report that it's not easy for books to compete with group trainings. But I have a dream for you and *Juicy Joy*. I fully intend for this book to be every bit as significant in your life's journey as the very best group training you could attend. So I'm going to share with you the two reasons that workshops are frequently more effective than books, and I'm going to tell you how to make sure your Juicy Joy experience is an exception to that rule.

When people come together with shared goals and a common intention for the highest good of all, it creates an amplified energetic field where amazing stuff can happen. Reading this book all by yourself in your room won't get you that particular advantage, so I want you to go right now to my website and join the free Juicy Joy online community. You can participate as little or as much as you want, but just joining will get you a bit of that group energy. To amp it up further, consider working through this book with a buddy or small group of friends. Do it with the real people in your life, or with partners in the Juicy Joy online community. Just click "hook me up" to join or form a group online.

The second reason group trainings can be more effective than books is this: In a facilitator-led group, you have to do the exercises. Someone is watching you, so you do them. The way around this is so simple and so obvious, but I still want you to imagine me jumping up and down right now, throwing a little fit in my insistence of it. Do the exercises! Do them right when I tell you to do them!

I know so many of you aren't going to do this, and it breaks my heart. I know because for fully the first ten years I spent devouring every personal-development book on the market, I didn't always do the exercises. Why? I don't know—there is no good reason why! I was just too lazy to get up and go get a notebook. Or I thought I already had the answers in my head and didn't want to slow down my progress through the book. Or I thought that particular exercise didn't apply to me, or I'd done it before.

None of these are good reasons! Even if you've done an exercise before, it could shed amazingly different light for you today. I had *favorite* books, ones that I quoted religiously and passed around to all my friends and acted like a smarty-pants authority on . . . and all that time I had *never* done the exercises in them. When I went back many years later and read these same books while fully completing each exercise, it was such a profoundly different experience that I vowed I would never waste an opportunity like that again. So, as you embark on your Juicy Joy journey, make yourself this promise: *I will stop and do the NakedWritings and JuicyFeels!*

The author Natalie Goldberg has a cake analogy I love. When you bake a cake, you have ingredients, right? You have eggs, butter, milk, sugar, and flour. The ingredients are the different parts of your life. You mix them all together in a bowl, but this doesn't make a cake. It makes goop. To turn it into a cake, you have to add the energy of intense heat. To turn your life into a life worth living, you have to add the heat and energy of your heart and soul! Otherwise it's just goop.

So there are two ways you can use this book going forward. You can read it; or you can *experience* it—by bringing the heat and energy of your glorious, gutsy self to all the personalizing processes I've created for you. Reading it will generate a dramatic, permanent shift in the way you view yourself and the world. If that's all you're looking for, you have my blessing to simply read.

But I'm hoping you want more. I'm hoping you choose to *experience* Juicy Joy . . . because, like Jack Kerouac said, "The only people for me are the mad ones, the ones who are mad to live, mad to talk, mad to be saved, desirous of everything at the same time, the ones who never yawn or say a commonplace thing, but burn, burn, burn like fabulous yellow roman candles exploding like spiders across the stars and in the middle you see the blue centerlight pop and everybody goes, 'Awww!'"

Be a mad one. Let's unleash your Juicy Joy.

STEP ONE

EMOTION-MIXING

I often read this stunning poem in Juicy Joy workshops. With Oriah's blessing, I share it with you now to kick off your journey into radical authenticity and self-love:

The Invitation

It doesn't interest me what you do for a living.
I want to know what you ache for,
and if you dare to dream of meeting your heart's longing.

It doesn't interest me how old you are.
I want to know if you will risk looking like a fool for love,
for your dreams, for the adventure of being alive.

It doesn't interest me what planets are squaring your moon.
I want to know if you have touched the center of your own sorrow,
if you have been opened by life's betrayals
or have become shriveled and closed from fear of further pain.
I want to know if you can sit with pain, mine or your own,
without moving to hide it or fade it, or fix it.

*I want to know if you can be with joy, mine or your own,
if you can dance with wildness and let the ecstasy fill you to the
tips of your fingers and toes without cautioning us to be careful,
to be realistic, to remember the limitations of being human.*

*It doesn't interest me if the story you are telling me is true.
I want to know if you can disappoint another to be true to yourself;
if you can bear the accusation of betrayal and not betray your own soul;
If you can be faithless and therefore trustworthy.*

*I want to know if you can see beauty even when it's not pretty, every day,
and if you can source your own life from its presence.*

*I want to know if you can live with failure, yours and mine, and still stand
on the edge of the lake and shout to the silver of the full moon, "Yes!"*

*It doesn't interest me to know where you live or how much money you have.
I want to know if you can get up, after a night of grief and despair, weary
and bruised to the bone, and do what needs to be done to feed the children.*

*It doesn't interest me who you know or how you came to be here. I want to
know if you will stand in the center of the fire with me and not shrink back.*

*It doesn't interest me where or what or with whom you have studied.
I want to know what sustains you, from the inside, when all else falls away.*

*I want to know if you can be alone with yourself
and if you truly like the company you keep in the empty moments.*

Can you sit with pain without moving to hide it, or fade it or fix it? Can you dance with wildness and let the ecstasy fill you up to the tips of your fingers and toes?

To access our full potential for joy, we first have to get comfortable with owning the spectrum of our feelings and acknowledging our duality. When we stop trying to suppress our emotions, and simply surrender to them, there is always perceptible joy there. This is juicy. This is real. This is the path to your true, authentic self.

Emotion-Mixing is the rare ability to truly welcome and embrace every emotion as it arises, judging none of them; understanding that seemingly conflicting emotions can coexist side by

side, without one having to overtake or cancel out the other. It's the salty-sweet of the chocolate-covered pretzel, the brilliantly written novel that leaves you laughing and crying at the same time. It's the key to a Juicy-Joyful life, because that insatiable itch you've been calling a longing for "happiness" is actually simply a longing to *feel*. We're so accustomed to pushing away our undesirable emotions that we don't even notice how our refusal to feel *certain* things results in our inability to feel *any*thing.

From the second we arrive on Earth, we're bombarded by dangerous information. Our parents pat our backs and say, "Don't cry." Why? Because crying means we're sad, and sad is no good. It's the first lesson we're taught, and it gets reinforced throughout our lifetimes. What if we hadn't ever learned that paradigm? What if our parents had gazed just as proudly and adoringly at our bunched-up, red, crying faces as they did at our beatific smiles? What if we were never taught a preference for happiness?

There is a richness and satisfaction in such "undesirable" emotions as sadness and anger—there's something in them that calls to our humanness. If that weren't true, we simply would not participate in those feelings. The anguish and suffering that come along with them are caused by our resistance to feeling them; our culture-created perception that these particular emotions are unacceptable and are somehow mistakes—things we should not have to feel.

You've been indoctrinated to believe that the smiley, giddy sensation of "happiness" is the only emotion worth living for, and that you have to reluctantly trudge through all the others while waiting for those "happy" circumstances to show up. But this step will show you why true, sustainable joy is only available when you learn to fully embrace every other natural human emotion under its banner.

Emotion-Mixing gives you the ability to flow, fully, with each feeling as it arises—those you label "good" as well as those you label "bad." It's riding the wave of each emotion so deeply that you naturally transmute it into a glorious force for expansion. When you've mastered Emotion-Mixing, there's nothing to resist, because you welcome it all. You embrace each emotional twist and turn with such poignancy—you surrender so fully to it—that the surrender itself becomes a powerful instrument of creativity.

Would you really want all your life circumstances to show up perfectly to your satisfaction at every moment? Would that result in happiness . . . or abysmal boredom?

Charles Augustin Sainte-Beuve said, "There exists in most men a poet who died young, whom the man survived." I know this poet. And I don't believe for a second that he dies, ever, in any of us. He might get buried . . . cryogenically frozen . . . but he's always there waiting for us to breathe life into him again. The poet-energy in each of us must now be revived and nurtured, because it is the only important thing about us. The rest of us is just elbows and organs and fluids, materialistic cravings and fears.

Compartmentalizing and labeling our emotions leads us to judge them and reject the ones we label undesirable. The ways we typically reject emotions are by denying them, struggling against them, or vainly attempting to abolish them altogether. This tendency can become magnified for those of us on a spiritual path, when we start to berate ourselves for every negative emotion, fearing that it will only draw more negativity to us. Sometimes it feels like we're supposed to make the garden of our emotions resemble the meticulous lawns at Disney World, with smiling topiaries shaped to perfection and not a weed in sight.

Maintaining your emotional garden to this degree is exhausting work. Let it grow free! Let it become an African plain, a Colorado mountainside, an Amazon jungle! Revel in the rich diversity of it, the surprises, the rawness! It's not the sad thought itself that attracts negativity; it's our resistance to feeling it. Emotion-Mixing is learning to love our sadness, find exquisite beauty in it, and be deeply thankful for the expansion and growth it can bring us.

Embrace Your Taijitu Nature!

This Emotion-Mixing Step has its roots in Buddhism and early Chinese philosophies, with the whole yin/yang, *taijitu* concept.

The taijitu is that round symbol you've seen a million times that looks like two sperm cuddled up in a ball; one black and one white, each with a dot of the other's color inside it.

Most Westerners associate the taijitu with good and evil, but Taoist philosophy actually pooh-poohs that kind of dichotomous moral labeling. It's really more about balance. For joy to exist there must be sorrow, or we'd have no basis for comparison. All of our desires are born out of contrast. We experience something we don't like, and that makes clear for us what it is that we want. Sometimes it's as black and white as the taijitu. Sometimes it's gray and murky. But every time we experience what we don't want, we're gifted with a clearer understanding and desire for what we *do* want.

Emotion-Mixing is maintaining an appreciation for the taijitu and that little dot of contrasting color in each spermish swirl. The image is designed to give the appearance of movement, fluidity. Its message is that in every experience we deem negative, there is a seed of positive, and vice versa. It's time for us to deeply understand that our negative experiences are the ones that afford us the most growth and expansion. We know that, intellectually, but until we deeply comprehend it, we won't get the knack of Emotion-Mixing. Whatever sucks for you right now is going to continue to suck until you find the dot of contrast in it—the opportunity to thank it for what it's taught you, so that you can move beyond it.

Radical authenticity means accepting that we *are* the taijitu. We love to present to the world that we are mostly one of the colors. And many of us secretly fear within our hearts that we are primarily the "negative" color. To be free, and to live in Juicy Joy, we have to proudly exclaim, inwardly and outwardly, that we are both, knowing it is right and good that we are both. Within the side we consider our weaknesses, there is that dot representing our strength. The totality of both sides, interconnected, is what makes us whole and human and magnificent.

Are you ready to claim your taijitu nature?

To illustrate Emotion-Mixing, I'll tell you about Laura, one of my students who was struggling with a long-standing mother issue.

Laura was a very sweet woman who had grown up with a mentally unbalanced mom who verbally and emotionally abused her and kept her perpetually focused on somehow winning the consistent, loving approval she so desperately craved. As an adult, Laura suspected that her unresolved issues around her mother were keeping her from trusting her relationship partners and achieving real intimacy, and she feared they were also blocking her from myriad other opportunities in life. She was right. Victimhood and unresolved relationships (particularly with parents) will do that.

Laura had been through many self-help programs and done buckets of forgiveness work. She told me she truly believed that she had forgiven her mother; she knew her mother had done the best she could, and she wanted to simply love her now. I inquired about the phrasing of "wanting to love." Laura's lip quivered as she explained that she still felt guarded in her interactions with her mom, and still felt angry and wounded in the now-rare instances of the woman's verbal attacks.

In my workshops, we sometimes make tea. It's an exercise to bring our understanding of Emotion-Mixing to an experiential level. I had Laura choose a tea bag for each of the emotions she recognized having toward her mother. I told her to be totally honest with herself, and hold nothing back. She quickly chose one tea bag labeled "sadness." The others she chose were labeled "fear" and "anger." I asked her if she'd like to add "love." She seemed relieved to have been given this option and readily added it to her collection.

After a bit of ritual and meditation, we all made our tea. Laura watched the colors swirl independently from each tea bag and then intermingle into one rich, dark, indeterminate shade. The goal of this exercise is to fully embrace and accept each of our sometimes disparate emotions as valid and worthwhile. All suffering comes from either denying or disliking some aspect of ourselves. When we honor every part of us, including the emotions we'd been denying or resisting, we heal.

For Laura, the truth was that there was a whole lot of love, and a whole lot of hurt. Focusing on the hurt as an excuse not to love was not the solution. Trying to deny that the hurt existed was not the solution. It's in our nature to love, and it's perfectly okay to love someone and be angry with her at the same time. Rather than negate one another, the different flavors can swirl together to create a vibrant new blend. It's not a bad cup of tea.

NakedWriting for Applying Emotion-Mixing

- In your Juicy Joy Journal, draw a circle the size of a small plate and divide it, like a pizza, into eight slices.

- Break down your life into eight different categories, however that makes sense for you. A typical breakdown might be: career, primary relationship, family, health, spirituality, leisure time, friends, and hobbies/interests. Label each slice accordingly.

- Look at one pizza slice and observe your immediate feeling when you consider that area of your life. Simply feel it; don't think about it. If you start making a mental list of pros and cons, then you're thinking, not feeling.

- Give that slice a rating, from one to ten, to describe how much joy you're feeling in that area of your life, ten being the highest amount of joy. Be super honest.

- Rate the rest of the slices. (Get ready to raise your score in each slice of your life as you work through this book.)

- Look at the areas with the lowest scores. What factors are contributing to those low numbers? Does it seem like the factors are out of your control? Isolate one of the circumstances that's causing a pizza slice to score low and write it in your journal.

Is there anything good about this circumstance? Is there anything you can find to be grateful for about it? Be honest. If you can't find anything good about it, that's fine. Tune into your body right now. Is it uncomfortable to direct your attention to this circumstance? Does it make you feel guilty? Anxious? Ashamed? Indignant? Angry? Frustrated? Fearful? The first thing you need to do is acknowledge the full truth of where you stand at this exact moment, so take the time to notice every emotion that applies.

Now spend a moment considering the possibility of the following crazy-ass idea: What if everything on your pizza is precisely as it should be? What if, instead of being uncomfortable with your negative feeling, you found a reason to love and celebrate it? Maybe that negative feeling is here right now to lead you to something wonderful.

What if the things you hate most about your current situation are your greatest blessings in disguise? What if everything that's ever unfolded in your entire life has been the precisely necessary thing to bring you to this mysteriously perfect moment? If that resonates at all with you, see if there's another emotion you can blend with what you're feeling. Can you blend in curiosity? Hopefulness? Enthusiasm to make some sort of change?

Think back to the times in the past when something in your life has really sucked. In hindsight, can you identify any ways those experiences have benefited you? Nudged you on to something great you might otherwise have missed? Helped you grow emotionally? Again, be honest. If you can't see it right now, that's fine. If you *can* see it, can you feel grateful now for those experiences?

Consider the possibility that this moment in time is no different from those. Is it possible that there will come a day when you will be grateful for the things you are now experiencing as unwanted circumstances? If that seems plausible, can you make the stretch to feeling grateful for them now? Gratitude is the most powerful emotion to practice blending with others. It takes the sting and suffering out of any emotion, freeing you to fully feel it.

Undoubtedly you've had hardships that felt impossible to be grateful for while you were in the thick of them. But in retrospect, isn't it easier to see that many of those hardships have brought you gifts in the long run? One gift that is often overlooked is the gift of contrast. Every time you experience something you don't like, you have the opportunity to form a clearer definition of what you do like and want for yourself. Think of the almost-cliché example of the cancer survivor who says that getting cancer was the greatest thing that ever happened to him because it helped him stop taking his health, his loved ones, and his very life for granted.

It Sucked, and I'm So Grateful

I deeply love all of my family members and cherish my relationships with them. I am able to look back and see nothing but the love I've exchanged with them because I've decided that none of the rest of it matters. But for the majority of my less-enlightened life, the "rest of it" was challenging for me. I'd done a lot of healing work when the most recent challenge surfaced. I could have sworn I was through. But the people who raised us often present the most powerful learning opportunities, and I was apparently still in need of one.

When I shared the news with two of my senior family members that I would be ending my 14-year marriage, I encountered some extreme dissention. Even though I knew it was ridiculous for a grown woman to continue allowing herself to be emotionally manipulated by her family of origin, and even though I'd done mountains of work already on my people-pleasing tendencies, their reaction still hurt. It caused a painful tension in my interactions with them for several months.

My coping mechanism has always been journaling, and one day as I was journaling about this situation, I realized the gift in it. The truth was that even though I had spent well over three years making every conceivable attempt to rebuild and justify my marriage, there was a part of me that remained uncertain I had done all I could. If that hadn't been the case, my family members' opinions simply could not have affected me.

The treasure in this painful rift was that it alerted me to those vestiges of lingering doubts, and put me in the position of definitively evaluating my decision. In doing that, I was able to recognize that my self-doubts were rooted in old, unloving patterns of putting myself last. That understanding let me get very clear within myself that I had chosen the right path, since I truly could not have been authentic in any other.

Had those two powerful people in my life only been politely disapproving, I would not have suffered as much, but I also might have subconsciously remained conflicted on some level, and allowed that conflict to paralyze my forward movement. The intensity of their disapproval of me, though hurtful, was actually a blessing.

By staying my course in the face of their disdain, I also got to prove to myself that I had mastered a certain level of self-love and authenticity. An additional gift was the opportunity to integrate even more deeply my understanding that my current definition of love is vastly different from the definition I learned from my family of origin, and in their own way, they were only demonstrating their love for me.

There is a further point to be made here, and it does push the woo-woo envelope, so be forewarned. I believe that if I hadn't needed this uncomfortable situation to unfold, it would not have. I've come to trust, implicitly, in a guiding power that I'll be referencing throughout this book. I know that every situation I face—whether a "good" one or a "bad" one—is a carefully selected gift from this guiding power I call the Universe. I deeply trust and believe that the Universe adores me and is constantly orchestrating on my behalf.

Knowing this gives me the room to blend good-feeling emotions into any bad-feeling ones that come up. It also gives me the room to allow myself to fully feel and express every emotion. If the Universe gives me something to get angry about, and I suppress or resist my anger, I'm basically wasting that precious gift from the Universe. Even when I'm completely clueless about what a positive outcome might be, I've learned, through trial and error, that every time I let myself have my feeling and express it completely, I'm led to something wonderful. There are no exceptions.

Thank You, Unwanted Pain

Your emotions are very real aspects of you. Denying and hating them is a form of self-loathing. You are an energetic system, and emotions are energies that reside within that system. To reach the Juicy Joy level of self-love, you must start loving and thanking every emotion you feel. Had I denied the pain I felt in the above difficulty with my family, or whined about the injustice of being made to feel it, I would have blocked its gift.

Even if you are among my many beloved friends I consider woo-woo impaired, you've probably heard about the Law of Attraction. The Law of Attraction is based on the principle that "like attracts like"—meaning, at its most simplistic level, that negative thinking will energetically attract negative events and situations to you and positive thinking will energetically attract positive ones. The Law of Attraction states that whatever you give your attention to will grow, good or bad. That's true, and for real, and not as woo-woo as you think.

Why then, would I be telling you to give in to your negative emotions? Because you're human and stuff is going to piss you off. You will have desires, and things will get in the way of those desires. The natural spectrum of emotions that are available to human beings includes some sucky ones. It would be great if we could simply decide not to feel them, but for most of us that just doesn't work.

Attempting to mentally override a natural emotion because you're afraid that it will draw bad things into your life causes that emotion to bury itself within your energetic body. You might successfully get it out of your *conscious* level of awareness, but the energy it takes to suppress it creates a vibration that is just as powerful as your conscious attention. From a Law of Attraction perspective, your vibrational frequency is what draws things to you. Your vibrational frequency is definitely affected by where you choose to place your deliberate attention, but unfortunately it is also affected by your undeliberate attention.

There's an iceberg model often used in psychology to illustrate the ratio of conscious thoughts to unconscious ones: Picture an iceberg. The bit sticking out above the waterline represents your conscious thoughts. The big-ass chunk beneath the waterline represents the energy of the beliefs you're storing that you aren't even aware of. When you deny any emotion, you're just shoving it down beneath the waterline. When an above-water belief conflicts with a below-water belief, you experience it as a vague, uncomfortable discord within you. It drains your energy and prevents you from beaming out clear vibrational signals to attract what you want.

Does it seem unfair to you that you'd be drawing unwanted circumstances because of beliefs you don't even have any conscious control over? If source energy is responsible for this Law of Attraction, and source energy is God, and God is love, then why is it set up so that we have to experience crappy stuff? To me, the obvious conclusion is that it would not be set up that way *unless* the crappy stuff was there to benefit us.

I deeply believe that our ultimate purpose is to feel joy, love, and expansion—and *everything* we experience is designed to bring us closer to that end. Knowing that there's a gift in every emotion allows us to keep our feelings above the waterline of our conscious attention so that we can blend them with gratitude and learn from them . . . which will always, unfailingly, lead us to greater joy, love, and expansion!

Does that mean I want you to keep having unwanted circumstances in your life? No. It means I want you to wake up and stop *resisting* them so that you can stop attracting them. They're not here to punish you; they're here to help you move to a greater realm of joy and love. It's up to you to figure out their message (you'll learn how throughout book), and once you do, you won't have to experience that particular flavor of unwanted circumstance again.

Can you imagine getting happily excited when things don't go your way? Having that much faith in the force that guides you? This kind of faith allows you to feel sadness, anger, and shame, but at the *same* time feel good about feeling those things. It allows you to mix those emotions with hope, optimism, and peaceful certainty that all is as it should be, and lets you know you are headed for better-feeling moments.

Celebrate contrast and thank it! Without it, you'd just be numb.

The Ever-Swinging Pendulum

Contrast is your friend. It gives you a broader emotional playing field to express yourself in. Deep down, you know it's true that some of the very worst things in your life were responsible for the very best things in your life. There's an overcompensation effect that happens when we allow ourselves to deeply feel our despair. The full expression of any negative emotion naturally gives rise to the desire and determination for a more positive experience. Depression and its more common sidekicks, like general malaise and boredom, are the result of this natural ebb-and-flow process getting interrupted; immobilized by our stubborn resistance to feeling.

A pendulum can only swing one way to the extent that it swings the other. For many of us, the pendulum of our emotions inches back and forth in pathetically tiny arcs. It's time to get over our fear of broadly swinging pendulums! Embracing your despair unlocks the gateway to feeling equally intense joy.

I've had students argue this point by insisting that they'd had plenty of despair yet still not seen the joy. But when they examined how welcoming they'd been of the despair, they realized that they'd been fighting against it and denying it and hating it the whole time, which means they were not allowing themselves the full experience and expression of their feelings. The biggest culprit here is the crazy, rampant idea that we should not ever have to feel bad. That idea is what leads us to resist and struggle against certain emotions, and the struggle is what actually causes our suffering, not the natural emotion itself.

I grew up without the ability to discover who I authentically was and express that to the world. It caused me considerable pain and suffering, and a period in my early adulthood of feeling lost and confused. But once I was able to clearly identify the problem —once I knew that authenticity and self-love were the things that were missing for me—I was able to focus on finding ways to have them. Once I got a taste of it, I wanted more. And more. And more. If you come by your authenticity easily, you probably don't think much about it, but I love mine with an ardent passion that makes me giddy. I appreciate it so much more than people who've never had to struggle for it.

Those people who have never thought to strive for extra authenticity are missing out on so much! I wouldn't trade places with them for anything! The enthusiasm born out of *contrast* is what led me to push my authenticity standards beyond what's simply comfortable into what's gloriously joyful! We come into each lifetime with a path—a soul plan. Mine, in this life, is to learn and teach ever-evolving levels of transparency and self-love. If I hadn't suffered deeply from circumstances pertaining to authenticity, I definitely would not possess the drive I have to embrace this path. Therefore, the suffering was a gift—one I'm grateful for every day!

The purpose of a life path, or any life lesson for that matter, is not to burden us with a heavy obligation. The purpose is to lead us to our greatest joy. The purpose is always joy. And the Universe (the energy that fuels the Law of Attraction) is always conspiring to help us get it. I like to say "the Universe." You might prefer to say "God," "Spirit," "Angels," "Guides," or "Higher Self." Just know that when I say "the Universe," I mean all those things.

Everyone has a life path that he or she is here to travel. We don't always understand the paths of others. We don't need to. We just need to honor those paths—every one of them. It's hard not to want to rescue, to repair injustices. And it's fine to attempt those rescue missions, if we can come from a place of first fully accepting the perceived injustices by recognizing they are a perfect and necessary piece of someone's life path. After fully acknowledging that, we can swoop in with our rescue efforts if that is indeed part of *our* life path. That is the only way to truly affect any change. Hating any circumstance and fighting against it will always, faithfully, cause it to grow. What we resist—*say it with me*—persists.

Accept, Accept, Accept

Acceptance is the key to Emotion-Mixing! But let your emotions flow freely with your acceptance. In some enlightenment practices, the goal is to become so accepting that nothing can ever disrupt your tranquility or set your pendulum swinging. This is not the Juicy Joy way. Instead, we accept the disturbing situation while also embracing the full force of every emotion it stirs in us. Honoring each of your feelings will keep you vitally connected to your inner voice, while allowing your emotions to flow freely through you without numbing you or causing you excess discomfort.

When we were little, our feelings came up strongly, and we felt them fully and expressed them full-out, right? We've all heard a kindergartner tell her best friend, "I'm mad at you, and I don't want to play with you!" Then five minutes later they're laughing, hugging, and picking each other's noses. Kids have it right; unfortunately, this gets beaten out of us. As we grow, we learn more and more ways to suppress our emotions, as well as whatever traits we learn are considered undesirable by those whom we depend on for love and our survival.

But suppressing those emotions causes them to fester into unnatural and unhealthy states like hate and depression. Hate happens when we compartmentalize our anger and blame someone or something for causing us to feel it. Depression happens when we compartmentalize and *deny* our sadness or anger. Mixing sadness or anger with other emotions, especially gratitude, allows them to flow through us in natural and beneficial ways. The parts we try to hide from the world are always the parts that keep us limited and stuck. All the energy we use to suppress these perfectly natural aspects of ourselves—if we could free it up, the amount of available life-force energy that would become accessible to us is staggering. We could literally create anything.

Over time, the resisted emotions that get stored within our energetic systems cause us much more distress than they would have caused if we had originally accepted them. They can cause us to become ill, have accidents, make poor choices. A common symptom of too many resisted emotions and beliefs is an overly busy mind.

Meditation helps silence an overactive mind so that stored energies can get unstuck and you can hear your inner voice. Meditating for even just five minutes a day can make you more receptive to that voice all day long. The more often you can meditate, and the longer you can do it each time, the sooner you'll start to hear your deeply buried authentic voice speaking to you. And what you'll hear it speaking, most likely, will be your true desires. Becoming your most authentic self will mean learning how to tune in to those desires, and how to bring to them to fruition.

NakedWriting to Blend Desire with Gratitude

- In your Juicy Joy Journal, list three things you're deeply grateful for in your life, right off the top of your head.

- One by one, vividly imagine each item on your list and allow yourself to feel sincere, deep gratitude for it.

- Now list three small things you want but don't yet have. (We'll get to the biggies soon!) Just three reasonable, relatively accessible goals—like a traffic-free drive to work, a desire for a meeting or project proposal to go your way, or a desire for your toddler to take a really good afternoon nap. Don't choose anything that's already a slam dunk, but don't make crazy requests either. Jot down whatever comes up for you.

Remember how we blended gratitude with our negative circumstances earlier by anticipating the day when the gift in the negative circumstance is revealed? In that same time-blurring way, see if you can blend genuine *gratitude* with the *desire* you feel for each of the things on this second list, as though they'd already gone exactly as you'd wanted them to. Feeling sincere gratitude for things that have not yet shown up in your life is the most powerful way to energetically attract the things you want. It feels good, and it removes the feeling of lack from the experience of wanting.

Go back and forth between the two lists, feeling gratitude for each item. Using both lists together will help you get clear on what the frequency of gratitude feels like so you can apply that same frequency-feeling to the things you're not yet experiencing. Continue to consciously bathe these things that have not yet occurred in your deep appreciation until the moment they show up. This exercise is a mini-version of what we'll soon be doing together. It will demonstrate your power to you and get you past your skepticism.

In Juicy Joy training, we learn to love the word *want*. When you can blend that feeling of want with the feeling of gratitude, every desire becomes juicy and exciting. Genuine gratitude in advance will never fail to bring you your desires.

How Good Can You Stand It?

Again, the reason you don't have everything you want in your life is this: You don't love yourself enough to believe that you deserve all the things you want. Even if that doesn't jibe with your conscious awareness—deep down, under the waterline, that's what's going on. The following NakedWriting and JuicyFeel will start to loosen up that subconscious anomaly so that you can work with it better in the coming steps. It will let you mix the emotions of your desires with the emotion of self-loving deservedness. As will often be the case in your Juicy Joy journey, the NakedWriting will customize the JuicyFeel for you.

You're going to spend a few moments making a mental list of the things you'd most like to contribute to the world, large and small. But this is important: *I do not want you to include anything on this list that feels like an obligation.* If you sigh inwardly or feel your energy collapse in any way when you think of a particular item, it does not belong on this list. If you believe that caring for your elderly aunt is your greatest act of contribution, but you hate caring for your aunt, do not list that. Sacrifice and contribution are not the same thing.

This is a list of what you're *excited* to contribute—what you find joy in giving and doing for others. It could be a job or a hobby, but it doesn't have to be. It could be a contribution that affects lots of people, or just one. It could be as simple as supporting your husband or wife or kids, or one particular kid who really needs it right now. It could be kindness toward animals, or a recycling effort to save the planet. Anything you love doing that benefits any person, creature, or nature, that's what you put on your list. It's fine if the list is super long, or if it has only one significant item.

Also—and this may get your pen moving faster—it doesn't have to be anything that's actually taking place in the real world at the moment. If you have a secret fantasy about painting that really speaks to your heart and ignites your passion, but you aren't doing it yet, you can *imagine* yourself creating gorgeous paintings that bring tears to the eyes of everyone who sees them, just spreading that beauty and awe all over the planet with your art. You're going for a visceral reaction here. Your subconscious isn't going to say, "Hey, wait a minute . . . you don't even own a paintbrush!" It doesn't know the difference, so long as you're feeling the passion of your contribution.

I'm reminded of a cartoon I clipped out of *The New Yorker* many years ago. It showed a man standing in the aisle of an airplane holding a gun in one hand and a notebook in the other, saying, "No one is going to get hurt. I just want you to listen to a few of my poems." The point is: it's okay if you don't currently have a receptive audience for the thing you most want to contribute.

Next you're going to think about everything you want from the universe. Money, love, passion, respect, adventure, anything—what would you like the world to give you? I want you to tune in to your body. Don't *think* this; really *feel* it. What do you want, deep down? Let your imagination wander, and be open to the idea that your soul-level desires might come as somewhat of a surprise to you. Again, this list could be lengthy, or it could have just one fervent desire on it.

NakedWriting: Your Contributions and Your Desires

- When you're ready, NakedWriting style, list your contributions to the world in your Juicy Joy journal.

- Next, feel into your most honest, raw desires and list them there, too.

You're going to use those two lists to create your first customized JuicyFeel. Get the free audio at **JuicyJoy.com**, or read through to the end of the exercise and then go into the JuicyFeel with as much vivid emotion as you can manage. I'm going to give you a visual image, but I want you to internalize it however feels right for you—you don't have to "see" it clearly in your mind, so long as you can vividly feel it.

JuicyFeel: You, on Top of the World

— Move your body in some way that feels good to you, putting all of your attention on your body and the nice sensations there.

— Take several deep, slow breaths and relax into alpha brainwave state, however you've determined works best for you.

— Imagine the earth as a large ball, about four times taller than you, and imagine yourself standing on top of it. At the top, where you're standing, is a beach, and your bare toes are being pleasantly sucked into the sand as the gentle waves lap up against your ankles. Your arms are outstretched.

— Bring to mind the contributions you wrote on your list, and begin imagining all those contributions flowing lovingly from

35

your right hand, however that looks to you. Feel the joy of contributing so much to the world. Feel the world's gratitude as you
imagine your contributions flowing all around this planet you're
grounded in. Immerse yourself in this experience for several minutes, really cranking up the joy and pride you feel about your contributions.

— Next, switch your emotional focus over to the left hand,
and imagine all the things you want from the world flowing freely
into that hand. Know without the slightest hesitation that you deserve to receive these things. Feel that you are abundantly receiving them in this very moment, and notice the gratitude it inspires
in you. This isn't wanting, or hoping. This is full-on *having*, with
all the palpable changes that evokes in your body chemistry. This
is so much fun to do.

I find it's best to focus for several minutes on only one hand
at a time, because switching back and forth requires mental agil-
ity, and the goal is to turn off thinking and crank up feeling. But
beyond that simple framework, there aren't any steadfast rules.
Trust whatever comes up for you. You might imagine actual ob-
jects going in and out of your hands, or perhaps symbols like dol-
lar signs and hearts.

Some of the more abstract things you want might be repre-
sented by a flow of light, whatever colors you imagine, or swirls of
pixie dust. You can designate a particular color or symbol to represent a particular desire by just imagining that color or symbol
while simultaneously imagining what that abstract concept feels
like to you. What does respect feel like? What does love feel like?
What does passion feel like? Get yourself totally pumped with the
feelings.

Symbolism is the language of the soul, so it's significant to
your subconscious mind that you're on top of the world, even if it
seems cheesy to your inner critic. Several ancient traditions reference the right hand as being the "giving hand" through which
you send your gifts out into the world, and the left hand being

the "receiving hand," so you're tapping into some soul wisdom there, too. But if you're left-handed, you may be more comfortable switching the roles of your right and left hands. Try it both ways and see what feels best to you.

Do you see how this kind of balanced visualization can poke holes in that subconscious cap you have on what you deserve? You're not just sitting there saying, "The world owes me." You're actively involved in making the world a better place. You're re-inforcing that idea for your subconscious mind. You're giving and you're receiving, in perfect balance.

And if you did take liberties with reality when you came up with something you're contributing, it's not like we're really try-ing to trick the Universe here. If you made up the contribution about being an extraordinary painter, for example, and you use this meditation on a daily basis . . . guess what? You're going to start painting. You won't be able to help it.

Do this JuicyFeel as often as you can. It's best, of course, to do it when you can be alone and totally relaxed. But don't save it for those times. Pull it out informally as well, making it your go-to daydream whenever your life provides the opportunity for one. Folding laundry, waiting in bank lines, exercising. It will be a powerful ticket to your Juicy Joy, but only to the extent that you make use of it.

Love Note to That Better-and-Better You

To further cement your burgeoning beliefs of deservedness, I want you to write an affirmation on your bathroom mirror with a crayon, grease pencil, or dry-erase marker so that its energy will blend with your perceived image of yourself and therefore lodge more deeply into your consciousness. (If you don't have anything appropriate for writing on a mirror or you just really hate the idea, make a sign to tape on your mirror.)

Every time you see the affirmation written there, look deeply into your own eyes as you speak it to yourself. Your busy mind

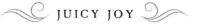
might try to tell you it's not true. If that's the case, deliberately still your thoughts until you can find the buried voice that knows it *is* true—the voice of your own source energy, your God-self. Pull that voice up and give it your full attention.

I'm going to start you off with a very powerful affirmation created in the late 1800s by the French psychologist Émile Coué, a pioneer of Law of Attraction principles before anyone called them that. Write it, say it, and believe it: *Every day, in every way, I'm getting better and better.* Your subconscious will apply "better and better" to any aspects of you that you believe need improvement, whether those beliefs are in your conscious awareness or not. From there, shift happens.

I chose that starter affirmation in case you're feeling shy about expressing love to yourself in a mirror. But once it feels comfortable, step it up. Write the most self-loving words you can bear to authentically speak to yourself, and keep upping the ante. Go to **LouiseHay.com** for daily suggestions from the goddess of self-loving affirmations, or buy one of her books. One of Louise's favorites (and mine) is simply: *Life loves me.* You want to choose words that truly excite you—even if it's just for a brief moment each time you see them.

Love Those Feelings

To know your feelings is to know *you.* Decide right now to honor and embrace every feeling that comes up for you. It takes practice because most of us are not in that habit. Start by simply setting the intention for yourself every morning when you wake up: "Today, I'm going to check in periodically and ask myself what I'm feeling." You might set a goal of deliberating observing your feelings at least once every hour. Then every time you look at a clock, let that serve as a reminder to check in with yourself.

Whenever you notice having a positive feeling, make a point to appreciate it. Your positive feelings are always a cause for celebration, and the more you celebrate them, the more you'll have. We'll be talking soon about the subconscious tendency we have, when we're feeling good, to caution ourselves against feeling *too* good. For now, just notice any moments you catch yourself doing that.

When you notice a negative feeling, consciously welcome that feeling, too. Invite it in. Observe how your default would be to resist the feeling, or push it away or deny it. Choose to do the opposite. Put your hand over your heart or your gut or whatever helps you to intensify the experience of the feeling. Mentally pull back into the "witness state" and observe yourself. Say to yourself, "How interesting that I'm feeling this right now." Doing this will remind you that you are not the feeling; you are separate from it. Ask the feeling what its gift is, and remain open for an answer to come to you, even if it doesn't right away. Try to feel grateful for the feeling.

My brilliant coach and friend Tej Steiner taught me this beautifully simple inquiry practice: As often as you can throughout your day, stop and ask, "What am I feeling right now?" After fully accepting and embracing whatever answer you get, next ask yourself, "What would I *like* to be feeling?" Directing your attention to what you want to feel (and vividly imagining that feeling) will naturally open up ideas and possibilities that will lead you to have the feelings you want.

The more comfortable you get with Emotion-Mixing, the easier it will be for you to welcome every feeling without resistance. And here's a big bonus benefit: Every time you welcome a new feeling that matches the energy of an old feeling you've previously repressed, you'll actually be *releasing* the negative energy that got stored in your energetic body with that repressed emotion.

The Sedona Method is one of the first trainings where I learned about the pockets of stuck energy we store in our bodies. There's a trick of this method I sometimes still use: When you feel a negative emotion, tune in to your body for a moment to see where you feel any kind of contraction or pain. Often it will be in your head, heart area, or gut, but not always.

It won't be apparent to you that this pain is related to the negative emotion you're feeling, but the discomfort is an indication that you've repressed this emotion in the past, and that is where it's gotten lodged in your energy body. As you now welcome this emotion, visualize a knot in the area of the contraction or pain. Shower it with your loving attention and see the knot gently un-raveling. When I do this exercise, I imagine that I'm mixing the negative emotion with the compassion and love of the God-self within me.

Emotion-Mixing, in a Juicy Nutshell

Practicing Emotion-Mixing lets you deeply relax into every emotion you feel. There's no need to resist anything, ever. And once you stop resisting, you'll automatically be headed in the di-rection of scrumptious, abundant Juicy Joy. Your good feelings are perfect because . . . well, because they're *good,* and feeling joy is what you're here for.

Your "bad" feelings are perfect, too, because they're always there to deliver a message that, when understood, will lead you to even more good feelings! Whether they're helping you get clarity about what you truly desire, preparing you for your soul's purpose, or deepening you as a person so that you can experience the ex-quisite richness of the passionate, meaningful life you signed on for—blending these "negative" emotions with heartfelt gratitude and acceptance is the secret to keeping the energy in motion and the pendulum in full swing.

We're all going to keep bumping up against our stuff. No mat-ter where you are on the path, if you keep evolving, you're going to keep hitting new layers to plow through. This is good and ex-actly as it should be. Learning to mix your emotions makes this never-ending process Juicy-Joyful.

I'll be honest. The whole Emotion-Mixing practice is much easier later in your Juicy Joy journey when you're already full-on adoring yourself. But *everything* is easier once you're loving your-self, and I had to make *something* Step One.

In Step Two, we're going to look at the mysterious metaphorical glasses we wear that cause every one of us to perceive the world in our own one-of-a-kind way. Most important, we'll discover where

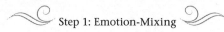

our own unique perceptions are serving our pursuit of Juicy Joy and where they're not, so that we can write the prescription for a fabulous new set of corrective lenses.

STEP TWO

FILTER-FIXING

I have promised to lead you to *you*. So it's time to look at the energetic membrane that separates everyday you from the glorious, gutsy self you truly are. I have come across this mysterious barrier in practically every training I've done, and I've come to recognize it as a very real and palpable entity—but one that thankfully proves to be malleable once we learn how to work with it. I call it your "filter."

Each of us has a built-in filter that determines our experience of reality. That's why two sisters might have dramatically different recollections of the exact same childhood event. It's why "beauty is in the eye of the beholder" and why there's great truth in Henry Ford's assertion that "whether you think you can, or think you can't, you're right."

Have you heard those stories about people who were present when a crime was taking place but didn't "see" what happened, and then years later they're hypnotized by a skilled hypnotist and can accurately report everything—every minuscule detail about the room—facts they had no conscious memory of whatsoever? They can do that because human senses are continually detecting and storing many, *many* bits of information—far more than our conscious minds can process.

You're constantly deleting perceptions and allowing other ones into your consciousness, and what gets deleted and what gets allowed in is determined by your filter. All the beliefs you've accumulated throughout your lifetime (conscious and unconscious) are what make up this filter. Filter-Fixing is the process by which we eradicate the beliefs that aren't serving you and enhance and magnify the ones that are. When you understand Filter-Fixing techniques, you can actually begin choosing what gets deleted and what gets allowed in.

It's been estimated that our senses register more than 7,000 bits of information every second. We're generally unaware of the vast majority of these impressions until one of them clicks into place with a conscious thought we're having (a thought that's in alignment with our beliefs). Even though we aren't aware of it, that's how every idea we've ever had was born. It might feel like an idea just bubbles up out of nowhere, but it's always the result of that linking-up system.

Our subconscious mind is truly all-powerful, and it has access to a staggering amount of data. But it's severely handicapped by the limiting beliefs we all have clouding up our filters. The more clearly you recognize the limiting beliefs that cloud your filter, the more apparent it becomes that your "reality" is a direct product of your perceptions.

I love the Tony Robbins exercise where he tells the audience to look around the room and make a mental list of everything that's brown. Then he tells them to close their eyes and yell out one thing in the room that's red. Of course, no one can think of anything red because they've just filled their minds with brown stuff. He instructs them to open their eyes and look for something red, and of course, they easily find things of that color. This is a brilliant way to demonstrate that, in any situation, what we find is what we're looking for. In that exercise, Tony has the audience members doing it consciously. But when we're not doing it

consciously, we're doing it unconsciously, and that means letting our filters control what we find and what constitutes our reality.

How Your Filter Got There

I'm sure you've heard someone say, "Well, in my world . . . blah, blah, blah." They're not kidding. Their world isn't your world, or mine, or anyone else's. Your world is nothing more than your perception of the world. Everything that's ever happened to you, every relationship you've ever had, and every place you've ever been . . . all of them have contributed to your one-of-a-kind filter. All of them generated feelings in you that caused you to form beliefs about the world and your place within it. Your filter is the grand sum of those interwoven beliefs. It never rests. It is fully operational every second of every day. It determines your response to every circumstance you encounter and every decision you make, from how you answer the phone to what kind of underwear you've got on.

You are reading my words right now, but your experience of these words is not identical to anyone else's experience while reading this book. None of us ever experience anything identically to the way another person does. I love this poem by Thomas Lux, which illustrates how our filters work:

The Voice You Hear
When You Read Silently

is not silent, it is a speaking-
out-loud voice in your head: it is spoken,
a voice is saying it
as you read. It's the writer's words,
of course, in a literary sense
his or her voice, but the sound
of that voice is the sound of your voice.
not the sound your friends know
or the sound of a tape played back

but your voice
caught in the dark cathedral
of your skull, your voice heard
by an internal ear informed by internal abstracts
and what you know by feeling,
having felt. It is your voice
saying, for example, the word barn
that the writer wrote
but the barn you say
is a barn you know or knew. The voice
in your head, speaking as you read,
never says anything neutrally—some people
hated the barn they knew,
some people love the barn they know
so you hear the word loaded
and a sensory constellation
is lit: horse-gnawed stalls,
hayloft, black heat tape wrapping
a water pipe, a slippery
spilled chirr of oats from a split sack,
the bony, filthy haunches of cows . . .
And barn is only a noun—no verb
or subject has entered into the sentence yet!
The voice you hear when you read to yourself
is the clearest voice: you speak it
speaking to you.

That voice in your head is not only there when you're reading. It's there all the time, the mouthpiece of your filter, and it's making those associations all the time. Since your filter is the lens through which you perceive the world, it is actually also creating the world you experience. It's that critically important.

Let's work that backward. Your life is made up of the different results you've created, right? What created those results? Your actions did. What created your actions? Every action is preceded by a thought. What creates your thoughts? Most of your moment-to-moment thoughts arise from triggers in the outside world. And all of those triggers come into your consciousness through your filter.

An Alternative Law-of-Attraction Hypothesis

The concept of Filter-Fixing provides a less woo-woo way to understand the Law of Attraction by suggesting that when you seem to start "drawing" or "attracting" positive circumstances to you, one explanation might simply be that you've begun perceiving the impressions and opportunities that would lead you to the things you want. Maybe they had always been there and you just couldn't see them before, because of the limiting beliefs that were clouding your filter.

Then it would stand to reason that when you're "attracting" things you *don't* want, it just means that you've been directing your attention to those things because your filter is programmed to allow only those corresponding perceptions through, due to limiting beliefs you've accumulated throughout your lifetime.

When you begin to fully *expect* to receive a particular thing you desire, you effectively rewire the limiting belief that was blinding you to the opportunities that would lead you to having this thing. The opportunities may have been in plain sight, but your filter was not allowing your perceptions of those ever-present opportunities to reach your consciousness.

For example, if you believe that success can only come after a long, excruciating period of hard work, then your filter cannot show you any opportunities for success until you've logged that sacrifice. But if you truly believed that you deserved wild success right now, then your filter would allow you to see the opportunities for that.

Even more woo-woo than the Law of Attraction is the metaphysical assertion that multiple realities are available at any given moment. But let's stretch our minds on this one for a second, too. If it's true that we consciously perceive a minuscule percentage of the "reality" that is available to be perceived in any instant (and it is), then it's easy to see how training ourselves to perceive what serves us best would indeed alter our experience of reality. One might say it would allow us to *choose* our reality.

A Brief Disclaimer

Remember in the Emotion-Mixing Step when we talked about how everyone has a soul plan to follow in this lifetime? To a large extent, your filter helps you fulfill this destiny. Even though it can lead you to unhappy experiences, as we've discussed, those experiences are often the keys to liberation and greater joy than you would have otherwise known. Your filter is not your enemy, and it's not something to try to get rid of (which would be impossible anyway). Take a moment right now to genuinely thank your filter for all of the experiences it's brought you—positive and negative.

You're reading this book, so I believe that you've come to some recent realizations about yourself and will come to many more realizations along your Juicy Joy journey. This is what the Universe wants for you. This is why you can clean up your filter now. Undoubtedly, there are some powerful forces in your filter at this moment that are blocking you from the things you want. You probably understand now that magically removing them would not work. The key to working with them is honoring the insights they're bringing you so that you can absorb their lessons and authentically replace the beliefs (conscious and unconscious) that put those forces there.

Sometimes just becoming aware of a belief will be enough to shift it. In the Bible, Saint Paul says, "Everything is shown up by being exposed to the light, and whatever is exposed to the light itself becomes the light." This is the alchemy by which digging up stuff we don't like about ourselves and exposing it to the light (fully acknowledging and accepting it) transmutes it into wisdom, freedom, and ultimately joy. Some beliefs have many layers that require additional work to allow them to shift. But when you fully understand how your filter operates, you'll have the incentive to do whatever it takes.

Your soul's plan does not need to be one of struggle. The lessons are only hard to learn when you fight against them. If you can train yourself to flow *with* each lesson as it unfolds, thanking it every step of the way, then "unwanted" circumstances in your

life will show up less and less frequently until you're barely experiencing them anymore. Part of getting into that flow is recognizing that everyone is on his or her own unique path, along with releasing the desire to control others' paths.

Here's the most extreme example I can give you: I was finishing up this book when my government killed Osama bin Laden. I couldn't help but ruminate on what his filter must have been like. Most likely, given the beliefs and life experiences that shaped his filter, he perceived a world in which he was a persecuted hero courageously fighting for a valiant cause. If that was what he perceived, then for this one individual, that *was* reality.

I don't mean to imply that he was blameless, or even that I objected to his murder. I know that whatever happens is exactly what is meant to happen, including that event. But I did feel such sadness for the Americans who rejoiced in it. Revenge is poison, and its toxicity damages those who harbor the revenge feelings, not those toward whom they are directed. Rejoicing in someone else's pain is always a sign that you are out of flow with your own soul's plan.

The cultures we grow up in are enormous contributors to the beliefs in our filters, and that's why people who are born in the same place and time often have many overlaps in their filters that allow them to share an "objective reality" that would not be shared by someone from a different time or culture. In the Story-Stripping step, we'll look closely at the rules we subscribe to that can limit us unnecessarily, many of which come from the time period and society we happen to be born into. Stepping outside of these "rules" in order to follow your authentic inner voice can be scary . . . and powerfully liberating, as we'll soon discover.

My Highly Controversial Jesus Theory

To illustrate just how powerful our filters are, I'm going to put forth my highly controversial Jesus theory now. From what I understand, there is very little known about Jesus Christ's childhood. Yet there seems to be quite a bit known about the night of his birth.

Here's what I think: Let's assume it's true that on the night Jesus was born, he was surrounded by people proclaiming him the Son of God and savior of humankind. Whether or not his parents ever overtly shared this information with the growing child (I believe it's assumed they did not), isn't it likely that there would have been leakage with information of that magnitude? Wouldn't this information cause his filter to develop in a significantly unique manner?

If his parents believed that Jesus had been singled out as a deity among men, born of immaculate conception, and if all the world was watching him with the expectation that he did not possess the commonly accepted limitations of human form, wouldn't the growing child sense that expectation, energetically, from everyone around him? Let's face it, the guy was probably pretty psychic. And if he *believed* all of that within himself, wouldn't he be tempted to test it out in increasingly spectacular ways? Wouldn't he be in a unique position to converse with God—source energy—and trust completely in the messages he received from God so that he could deliver those messages with the utmost conviction?

And if *the average child born today* were raised in such a way that his filter developed around the belief that he, above all others, had a direct connection to God and was capable of performing absolute miracles . . . isn't it conceivable that this child, too, would grow up conversing freely with divine energy and would one day be capable of walking on water, parting seas, and multiplying fish, if that's what he set his mind to?

I don't intend any blasphemy, and I'm not trying to say that Jesus wasn't the son of God. But wasn't his message that we're all children of God? And wasn't there something about "what I do, you can do and more"?

Belief is everything. The untapped secrets of human potential may very well be staggering and beyond anything we can imagine. But the only way for us to begin to unleash that hidden potential is to first believe, deeply, that we are capable of far more than we realize.

Let's Fix Your Filter for Self-Perception

Changing the beliefs that make up your filter will change your life. We'll be rewiring those beliefs throughout your whole Juicy Joy journey, but we're going to start with a few of the biggies now. Let's first look at the beliefs you have about yourself. Is there anything about you that you'd like to be different?

NakedWriting: Lists About You

- In your Juicy Joy journal, make a "Don't Like" list of all the things you don't like about yourself or wish were different. Include aspects of your personality, physical appearance, whatever mental or emotional weaknesses you consider yourself to have.

- Then make a "Like" list of all your strengths and the things you genuinely appreciate about yourself.

Look at the items on each list. Which list has more items that you spend a lot of time thinking about and giving attention to? You're more focused on the first list, aren't you? Doesn't it make sense that these aspects of you would be glaringly present in your reality, given all the attention they've been getting from you?

These two lists are showing you what's in your filter regarding your perception of yourself. The things on your "Don't Like" list are there because you've had some situations or relationships in your past that lodged judgments of those things in your filter. Period. They are not true in any objective sense of the word. They're showing up as "real" in your physical world for no reason other than the fact that they have taken up residence in your filter and you have nourished them with your attention. So let's shine that filter up a bit, 'kay?

Take the list of things you love about yourself and add to it, but this time, don't be restricted by "reality." Add any attributes you wish you had. To fully clear your filter of the items on your "Don't Like" list, you'll need to reverse each of them by putting its opposite on this list. For instance, if you have "clumsy" on your "Don't Like" list, add "graceful" to your expanding "Like" list. Make the "Like" list as long and luxurious as you want, adding whatever is important to you. You can include personality traits such as confidence or kindness; physical traits such as fitness; and external labels such as job title, marital status, or education achieved. This list defines your best self, precisely as you would like to be.

Done? Okay, now stretch your mind for a moment and see if you can wrap your head around this crazy-ass statement: *Your best self is your true self.*

This "Like" list came from your deeper consciousness, your spirit aspect. It's in alignment with what you believe would bring you the most joy, therefore it's part of your soul's plan—the plan that the Universe is always helping you out with. This ideal you is your soul-self, the you that's been around since the big bang or whatever you believe started it all. It's the you that you were when you came into this life, and the person you're meant to exit this life as.

The version of you with all those judgments on your "Don't Like" list is a far more recent creation; it's clearly the impostor. So now, I'd like you to do the following:

1. Cradle your journal up next to your heart as though it were a baby or puppy or something implicitly lovable.

2. Thank the things on your "Don't Like" list for all the opportunities for growth they have provided you. Thank them for showing you the contrast that is now allowing you to clearly focus in on your true, authentic self.

3. Imagine that you're watching the energy you had stored in those judgments move out of the words you wrote on the "Don't Like" list. That list is devoid of energy now.

4. Imagine the powerful energy settling into the words you added to your "Like" list to represent their opposites. Those words are now charged with the newly freed-up energy. It is done.

Open your journal and read all the items on your "Like" list again. They describe the true you. If you'd like to experience your day-to-day reality as that version of you, you can make that happen much more easily and quickly than you think. It's simply a matter of working with your filter, so let's do that now.

JuicyFeel: Mirror You

This JuicyFeel will be one of the most important ones you do, so set aside plenty of time and make sure you won't have any distractions. Since you'll be returning to it often, consider downloading the audio version at **JuicyJoy.com**. The subliminal messages on the audio will powerfully redesign your filter while your conscious mind enjoys the scrumptious fantasy journey. (If you prefer to do it on your own, read through to the end of the JuicyFeel and then create the scenario vividly in your mind.)

— Move your body in delicious, pleasing ways, focusing all your attention on your movement.

— Take several deep, pleasurable breaths and relax yourself into alpha.

— Imagine yourself in the most beautiful, peaceful, perfect nature setting you can dream up. Whatever emerges for you is just right. You might be on a beach, in the mountains or woods, or in a gorgeous meadow. You are completely alone, the weather is spectacular, and you are delighted to have this time for yourself. I like to be naked for this one, but if that freaks you out, suit yourself up in some comfortable, minimal attire.

— Walk along in this idyllic setting until you see, off in the distance, a large, ornate mirror. You're so happy to see it because you know it is the Mirror of Truth, where you'll get to see your most authentic self.

— As you get closer to the mirror, allow your thoughts to drift to the items you wrote on your "Like" list and feel the flutter of excitement, knowing that you are all those things and that is what you're going to see reflected. Anticipate seeing your physical self exactly as you want to appear. You might be dressed for your dream occupation or hobby. But you'll see so much more than that as well. In your eyes, and in the way you stand and carry yourself, you'll see the courage, the confidence, the integrity, and all the other intangible attributes you wrote down.

— Step up to the mirror and bask in the brilliance of the glorious Mirror You reflected there. This version of you clearly possesses every trait on your "Like" list and then some. Smile broadly. Hug yourself. Do a little twirl; or if you're a dude, do some manly pose. Feel the truth of what you're seeing.

— Look deeply into your eyes and feel how incredible you are. Say to Mirror You, "I love you madly." This is *your* ideal version of yourself, so there's no reason not to feel enormous, abundant love, right? If you're having trouble loving yourself through and through, tweak Mirror You until you can feel it.

— Think of the attributes on your list and, to the best of your memory, say, "You are so strong," "You are so brilliant," or whatever else you'd written. Say it adoringly with deep feeling, as you would to a cherished lover. Don't worry about remembering every attribute on your list. The ones that occur to you are the ones you need to say.

— Stay here with the mirror for as long as you like. Be playful and affectionate with Mirror You. Dance and shimmy. Blow yourself a kiss. I sometimes like to lean my forehead against my reflected forehead and just be still with the love and appreciation.

— When you're ready, turn your back to the mirror and imagine Mirror You stepping out of the mirror and into your physical body. Wiggle your hips as you relish the tingly sensation of this energy slipping into your form, bringing vitality and aliveness to every cell. Know that a real energetic process has occurred and you truly are now this beloved, authentic version of you. Dance around in your nature setting, basking in the delicious energy of your wonderfulness.

— When you're ready to leave the JuicyFeel, find a spot in this lush imaginary world where you can assume the exact same position your physical earthbound body is currently in. Gently allow yourself to shift your awareness back into the room. Smile, knowing that the energy you've brought back with you is now at work *within* you, and a shift in your outer circumstances is irrefutably inevitable.

You *Are* Mirror You

You'll be returning to the Mirror You JuicyFeel and adding to it throughout your Juicy Joy journey. For now, spend as much time with this process as you possibly can. Do this instead of watching TV or stalking your friends on Facebook. Do it as you fall asleep at night, and in the morning as soon as you wake up. The more you do it, the more natural it will feel and the more you'll look forward to it. You'll probably want to make adjustments and tweaks here and there. Go ahead. Let Mirror You evolve into ever-widening realms of fabulousness.

Think about Mirror You throughout your day. Think about how exceptional it feels to be that You, and little by little, you will become more and more like Mirror You in your daily life. It will be a natural, easy process. You won't have to struggle to make the changes. You'll be led by your joy—not by some nagging, guilty sense that you need to improve yourself.

The more vividly and more frequently you do this exercise, the sooner you'll be able to clean up your filter so that Mirror You is the you perceived in the world of form as well. The transformation may be gradual, or astonishingly abrupt. The speed with which it comes about will be determined by the strength of your belief that Mirror You is the true representation of your most authentic self.

It's possible that your internal qualities have already shifted into perfect alignment with those you selected for Mirror You. External, physical qualities take a little more time. Inevitably, you will encounter evidence that your physical reality is not yet a match to Mirror You, so don't resist those moments or allow them to derail you.

If, for example, you weigh 180 pounds and Mirror You weighs 130, it will take a bit of time for reality to catch up. If you faithfully do this process, you will naturally, joyfully be led to take the actions that will bring you to your desired weight, but in the meantime you must not allow yourself any negative thoughts about your body. It's imperative that you feel yourself at the weight you want to be, and pay no attention to any evidence from the scale or your jeans to the contrary. It takes dedication to overcome habits of self-judgment, but it is so worth the dedicated effort. You must start loving and honoring all parts of yourself, even while some of those parts are still in the process of transformation.

This JuicyFeel works on all levels, even for your health and physical appearance. You will see spontaneous changes in your body, and you must celebrate them along the way. There are scientific reasons for the ability our minds have to alter our bodies, but the real science-y jargon makes my brain hurt, so here is the basic gist: In every moment, millions of the cells in your body die and are replaced by new ones. In fact, according to spiritual master Deepak Chopra, you have a completely new liver every six weeks. You have a new skeleton every three months, and every month you have a completely new skin. One year from now, every cell that is currently in your body will have died and been replaced by a new one.

Each cell of your body contains a tiny blueprint for your entire being; that's how cloning is possible. Cells, when examined microscopically, consist mostly of empty space, or *energy*. Your beliefs provide the energy that determines the blueprints for these cells— the cells are just tiny containers for the energy of your beliefs! The only reason that your body continues to look the way it always has (and the only reason it looks older every year) is because *you expect it to.* Change your beliefs; change your cells; change your body.

That is why, done regularly, this JuicyFeel will train your filter to get you the spectacular results you want.

Try to tap into its energy every time you look into a real mirror. Look deeply into your own eyes, recognize the true you within, and send yourself appreciation and love. If you find yourself too distracted by a not-yet-there physical reflection looking back at you, try squinting until everything's a blur except the eye-to-eye connection.

Juicy Embodiment Practice: Hip-Wiggle

In your Mirror You JuicyFeel, when your ideal self stepped into your physical body, didn't it feel good to wiggle your hips, even just in your imagination? Moving your hips opens up your vitality center—known in Japanese martial arts as your *hara,* and it also stimulates your third chakra, which is the chakra associated with self-love. Wiggling your hips is a quick shortcut to feeling juicy!

An association has now been made in your subconscious between wiggling your hips and being your best you. Every time you do this JuicyFeel and imagine the hip-wiggle moment, you'll further anchor that association so that eventually wiggling your hips in real life will bring on the full energy of the JuicyFeel for you.

Start wiggling your hips as often as you can to tap into the self-loving energy of Mirror You! Wiggle them every morning when you wake up and every night before you get in bed. Wiggle them every time you take a bathroom break! Wiggle them in whatever way feels most juicy-wonderful to you. I adore the sensuous feeling of the belly dancer's figure-eight hip movement, but experiment and see what kind of hip sway you love best.

How Were You Taught to Define Love?

Think back to your earliest memories of your family of origin. How did your family members express love to one another? To you? This is the definition of love you were taught in your most formative years—the definition that was programmed into your filter. If it's serving you well, by all means hold on to it. If not, it may be time to formulate your own definition from your now-broader adult perspective.

My student Lucy's biggest breakthrough in her Juicy Joy training came when she realized that she had internalized a severely distorted definition of love. She had long known that her mother had suffered from an undiagnosed narcissistic personality disorder, and Lucy felt that she'd dealt sufficiently with its effects on her through many years of therapy. But she hadn't ever examined how her whole concept of love was based on the love this emotionally wounded person had modeled for her.

Lucy's mom had frequently expressed love for Lucy with ardent, over-the-top language, telling her that no one could possibly love her as much as she did. But if ever Lucy said something that contradicted one of her mother's opinions, or if Lucy failed to sufficiently praise and adore her, her mom would "ice over," to use Lucy's words. She'd become scornful and punishing and Lucy would feel the complete withdrawal of her mother's love. Since this was the day-to-day love she experienced, Lucy naturally internalized it as the normal way that love is expressed. After all, her mother had told her many times that no one would ever love her as much as she did.

Understandably, adult Lucy was having relationship difficulties. So much of what we experience as romantic attraction is determined by our childhoods. Until we've recognized and healed those patterns, we're doomed to repeat them. Even though her mom's mental illness was a factor, the main glitch in Lucy's filter was one that is common to many people: Because her basic emotional needs were not met in her childhood, yet she was told that she was loved, she equated love with the feeling of not having her needs met. Young children have no choice but to accept at face value the definitions their caregivers provide them. Lucy's emotional interactions with her mother had been labeled as love, so they became her definition of love.

Consequently, adult Lucy repeatedly found herself with men who, for one reason or another, were not able to meet her needs. A perfectly wonderful man who was 100 percent capable of meeting her needs would not have stood a chance with her. He simply would not have been attractive to her because what he was energetically offering would not have jibed with her deeply ingrained definition of love.

Lucy beamed when she explained to the class that she now understood that her mom had never loved her at all. I tried to soften it by suggesting that she had loved her in the most complete way she was capable of. But Lucy instinctively knew she needed to believe that her mom had not loved her, because only then could she dissociate the energy of her relationship with her mother from the definition of love. It was a profound moment of understanding for her; such a relief to be freed from that distorted definition.

As long as Lucy subscribed to the definition of love she'd learned from her mother, there was no chance for her to experience a love that encompassed feelings of safety and consistency; the kind of love that comes from a whole, complete, self-loving person who wouldn't need Lucy to always agree with him and constantly praise him in order for him to keep loving her. She couldn't even imagine the possibility of that kind of love until she got clear about how distorted her childhood definition had been. She needed to label that childhood experience "not love," in order to be free to formulate her new, healthy definition.

Not only did Lucy's epiphany open her up to healthy adult relationships, it actually improved her relationship with her mom as well. Her mom's "icy" periods stopped hurting Lucy nearly as much as they once had, and she began to appreciate that the times her mom was overzealously pouring on the affection were the times that she was really trying, in her own limited way, to express genuine love.

Lucy realized she didn't need to *get* the exact, healthy kind of love she wanted in order to *give* her mother that kind of love. Giving it, authentically, from her heart, felt wonderful to Lucy. Remember when we talked about how the gift in an undesired situation can sometimes be the tendency to overcompensate in that area, so that the challenge can actually propel us to a much more fulfilling place than we would have landed in if the undesired situation had never existed? Thanks to her challenge with the definition of love, Lucy was led to discover the truest, purest sense of love—a kind of love most people never evolve enough to experience.

In Buddhism, it's called "metta" or loving-kindness, and it means finding the most giving, loving place in your heart and projecting that love onto everyone, and most especially onto the people who least inspire it in you. People you feel have hurt you and treated you unkindly are the very best recipients of this loving energy.

Expressing loving-kindness to others will always strengthen your self-love muscle, but expressing it toward those you feel wronged by will strengthen that muscle tenfold. And the more deeply you truly love yourself, the easier it is to be grateful to anyone who was involved in your path to becoming who you are! Without them, you would not be you.

Some people believe that we choose our parents before we're born. If that seems plausible to you, consider the possibility that you actually selected whatever challenges you've encountered because you knew they would best prepare you for your soul's path. Perhaps you needed to experience the contrast of those events so it could lead you to reach for something so much bigger and richer.

NakedWriting: Love Defined

- Take a few moments to NakedWrite in your journal any thoughts you have about the definition of love you learned from your family of origin, and how well or poorly that definition has served you.

- If you feel inspired, write a new definition now. Intend that this new definition replace whatever definition has been at work in your filter.

- Next, write any insights about why you may have chosen your parents and your childhood challenges, and how those challenges have shaped you.

The Truth about Love

Most people's filters are clouded by some inaccurate beliefs about love. We're going to work on that, but first we're going to do a little exercise together.

I want you to take a few deep breaths, shake out your shoulders, roll your head around, get really comfy. I want you to suck in all of the attention you've got stuck in the past, suck back all the attention you have scattered in the future . . . and then drop that big ball of your energetic presence, right down into your heart center. I'm not talking about the organ that is your heart; I'm talking about that energetic space in our bodies that we call our heart.

I want you to imagine opening your heart, as wide as you can, however that feels for you. Have you got your heart open wide? Now imagine the flow of love.

I'm going to ask you a question now, and I want you to answer it silently and truthfully, with the very first response that comes up for you. Imagine the flow of love. In which direction is the love flowing?

My guess is that you feel love pouring *out* of your heart. You might have automatically called up an image of your kids or your pet or your beloved, but I want you to really feel how easy it is for you to pour love out into the world this way. For many of us, this is just our default setting. I love to love, and I could always easily imagine just globbing love out all over everyone.

But when I started developing my Juicy Joy trainings, I realized something interesting. So I want you to stop imagining the love flowing out of your heart for a moment. Instead, imagine love flowing *into* your heart. Pause long enough to really imagine that.

Is it as easy for you to imagine? If you were able to imagine it, how does the flow feel? Does it have the same volume, the same energy, the same intensity as the love you sent out? For many of us, this is a real eye-opener. It certainly was for me.

It's harder to imagine the love flowing in, isn't it? I realize that it might be tempting at this juncture to point to the people in your life and say, "They're not loving me enough." But guess what? No one can give you more love than *you* are equipped to receive. And that amount is *not* determined by how much love you want. You could want mountains of love, but if you can't close your eyes and imagine love pouring into your heart like a tidal wave and *feel* what that would feel like, there's no way anyone can give it to you.

Love is energy, and you are an energetic being—so *you* control the traffic in and out of your energy field. Most people are controlling it *un*consciously. You're going to learn how to control it consciously. Many of us have had painful experiences when our hearts have been wide open. Our protective instinct to close our hearts to receiving love is so common and understandable. But it doesn't serve us.

This is the biggest lie people carry around in their filters about love. We have this misperception that the only thing we can control is how much love we *give*. We think it's up to other people to decide how much love we get. It's not. That's the lie. We are actually in charge of how much love we receive.

Practice imagining love flowing into your heart. Start with whatever feels comfortable for you, and then gradually build it up. Call to mind the people you already know love you. Deeply feel what receiving their love feels like, and then amplify it in your imagination. Allowing or inviting someone to love you isn't selfish or greedy. All of our hearts want to give love. Letting someone love you to the best of his or her ability is the kindest thing you can do for that person. Pretend that your heart is a giant vacuum, and practice sucking in love from everyone you encounter. Your family, the bank teller, the kid who delivers your pizza.

You're not pouting and demanding people's attention—that kind of behavior comes from a *closed* heart. You're joyfully, gratefully, allowing the natural love that exists everywhere to flow graciously toward you. And when you do that, you don't even have to think about sending love to others. You'll be doing that automatically. When you fill up with love like this, you're a love fountain. It will ooze out your pores. You will *be* love.

That's why I'm much more interested in teaching you to *receive* love than I am in teaching you to give love. Loving yourself is as simple—and as crazy difficult—as granting yourself access to the abundant flow of love that's always available. Let's do some Juicy-Feels to reprogram your filter in the category of love.

JuicyFeel: Filling Up with Divine Love

If you're a seasoned meditator, or if you've done some spiritual dabbling, you may already have a process for filling up with Divine Love. If you do, and it's working for you, stick with that. I've come across lots of different methods, but here is what I've developed that works best for me:

— Imagine God (or the Universe or Source or Spirit) as a brilliant, sparkling, iridescent white plasma. Since divine energy is all around us and within us all the time, imagine that you can simply draw this plasma from thin air whenever you care to summon it. You know that God is love, and God is there in everything you come in contact with, so it's just a matter of using your imagination to switch over into a visual and kinesthetic representation of that energy.

— Relax your mind and imagine this thick, rich, white, gooey substance flowing down into your body through the top of your head (through your crown chakra, for the woo-woo initiated). The glowing goo feels so warm and juicy and fabulous as it oozes down, down, filling every cell of your body, powerfully nourishing you with the purest form of unconditional love.

— If you're comfortable with the idea that your energetic form extends several feet beyond your physical form, you might want to imagine the sparkly plasma filling this extended version of you. But if that idea is a stretch, just let the goo fill your physical body.

Divine Love vs. World Love

You can choose to fill up with Divine Love anytime at all. God loves it when you do.

And some spirituality practices would stop right there. If the purest, best, most incredible flavor of love is always readily available to every one of us, why would we care about any other flavor?

Because it's fun. Because it's juicy. Because we chose to be here in this human form and every one of us has, at the top of the checklist on our soul's plan, to love one another.

World Love includes the kinds of love you feel for your red-hot soul mate, your best friend, your cockatoo, fresh raspberries, a half-price shoe sale, and the reflection of moonlight on a glassy lake. It feels different from Divine Love. Divine Love feels soft, safe, and protective. World Love feels exotic, unpredictable, thrilling, earthy, wondrous, dazzling, splendid, dangerous, miraculous, reckless . . . but good, good, good. World Love's got an edge to it. That's what makes it so exciting. When we expect World Love to consistently feel exactly like Divine Love, we're in for disappointment. We need to clear that expectation from our filters.

NakedWriting: What Do You Love?

In your Juicy Joy journal, make a quick list of things you appreciate. Do it haphazardly, off the top of your head. Who are the people you care about? What brings a smile to your face? What's your favorite food, favorite hangout spot? What makes you laugh?

Appreciation is love. You love these things, probably in vastly different ways and to varying extents. Since you're reading this in your human form, the love you express is World Love. Your filter is dictating the way you give and receive World Love, so let's see if we can adjust that a bit in the direction of your Juicy Joy.

JuicyFeel: Filling Up with World Love

— Stretch, move, and get your attention in your body.

— Breathe yourself into alpha.

— Allow yourself to fill up with Divine Love, either by using the guidelines I just introduced or however is familiar to you. Really saturate your consciousness with the abundance of this phenomenal love, until it feels like it needs to burst out of you through your heart center.

— Think about the things you just wrote in your journal, and observe the different kinds of love flowing from you to all of these things. You filled up with Divine Love, but the love you send out is World Love. World Love has Divine Love as its basis. World Love is Divine Love tinged with humanness.

— Let your love for all of these things take on different characteristics in your imagination—different colors, textures, degrees of chunkiness. Let's say you love your family, your home, your community, nature, animals, your romantic partner. Imagine that the pure, white Divine Love takes on a different color when it becomes your love for each of these things. Maybe your crazy-sexy, passionate love for your partner is red; maybe your love of nature is green, your love of your favorite hobby is blue, and your love for a child is pink. Don't let yourself get caught up in specific labeling; just let that idea guide your imagining so that you feel a rich, vibrant rainbow of swirly, tie-dyed, textured World Love flowing from your heart. Doesn't it feel glorious to love so much? See if you can crank up the flow to a passionate gush.

— Once you can vividly imagine that feeling, incorporate it into the JuicyFeel called You on Top of the World, which you learned in the Emotion-Mixing Step. Remember how you imagined sending your contributions out into the world from your right side? Now *add* the flow of love from your heart to all the things in the world, so that the love intermingles with the flow of your contributions.

— When you get to the receiving part, imagine not only that you are receiving the things you want into your left hand, but also that you're feeling World Love pouring fervently into your wide-open heart from all the beings and things you're now allowing to love you. Allow nature to love you. Allow the billions of people you've never met to love you. Think of the question that Einstein claimed was the most important question of all: "Is it a friendly universe?" This JuicyFeel will leave no doubt in your conscious-ness about the answer, as you blissfully receive all that yummy World Love rushing into your open heart.

Watch Where You Point That Thing

The seed for the Filter-Fixing step was planted many years ago during a Starbucks conversation with my fabulously juicy friend Rob Mack, an extraordinary life coach and the author of *Happiness from the Inside Out*. I had asked Rob his thoughts about the web of beliefs that uniquely determines how each of us perceives the world, and he responded with the most lovely camera analogy. He said that it's all a matter of where you point the camera. Until that moment, it had not occurred to me that our perceptions were within our control. How thrilling!

It's time for you to start retraining *your* filter by becoming de-liberately selective about what you allow through. You can let in fear or you can let in rapture. Make your perception-camera a mag-net for joy and love and juice. Wherever you are, whatever you're doing, you decide where to point the camera, where to zoom in, where to sharpen the focus, and where to deliberately soften it.

Valuable impressions that lead to Juicy Joy can be found ev-erywhere, and in the coming steps, you'll be training yourself to see them—just like you might train yourself to recognize the 3-D image hidden in a pattern. When you use your powers of perception like a camera lens, boundaries melt, labels lose their meanings, and breathtaking beauty abounds.

Learning to block out the extraneous perceptions that distract and limit you will naturally lead you inward, toward the true, authentic you. Like Paul Gauguin, who said, "I shut my eyes in order to see," you will unearth the inner voice of your own clear knowing.

Nancy Levin describes this kind of selective awareness in the following poem from her stunning debut collection, *Writing for My Life . . . Reclaiming the Lost Pieces of Me:*

> *immersing and emerging*
>
> *i watch her swim*
> *away from fear*
> *toward a sea*
> *free from restraint*
>
> *she does not look up*
> *or around*
> *only within*
> *breathing in and out*
> *immersing and emerging*
>
> *criticism crawls*
> *out of her body*
> *as she glides*
> *into a confident sheath*
> *peace ignites her core*
>
> *for the first time*
> *she understands awareness*
> *by being seemingly unaware*
>
> *standing now she rises*
> *her flesh propelled by*
> *bone muscle tendon*
> *blood is rushing her*
> *heart awake*

all love begins
with self-love
once you know
you are the root
of your own suffering
choose to disengage
from the periphery

harness and recognize
the strength inside
to magnetize

breath is the private mantra
guiding prayer
follow your feet knees hips
belly heart hands
be willing to lose your balance
surrender to what matters most
and dive into the unknown

Filter-Fixing in a Juicy Nutshell

Are you ready to dive into the unknown?

Perception is everything. There is nothing in this world that exists for you independent of your perception of it. Your filter is the energetic membrane that determines which perceptions—out of the thousands available to you in any given moment—land in your consciousness as your experience of reality.

Your filter is made of the energy of the beliefs you've accumulated and stored throughout your life. When a perception matches a belief you hold, you experience it as truth. Some of your beliefs are serving you and some are not, so the next two steps will focus on weeding out the beliefs that are causing you to experience the world in ways that prevent you from living as your most vital, glorious, joyful self.

In these steps, we're going to be working with some unflattering facets of your filter, and it's going to be imperative for you to understand that your filter is not you. You'll need to hold the vision of Mirror You as the true you, while we continue our work to clear away the debris that's been clouding your filter and distorting your options. Although we've powerfully redesigned your filter in several critical areas, the more time you spend with your JuicyFeels, the more transformational their results will be.

A client once complained to motivational guru Zig Ziglar, "All this positive thinking stuff is great, but it doesn't last." Zig replied, "Neither does showering. That's why I do it daily." There is no excuse, ever, to be without love. Divine Love especially—it's always available, so it's the easiest kind to fill up with. Whenever you feel low on love, just ask, and it's there. It will fill you up so that you can start blasting it back out, putting your earthly spin on it.

Every time you shower, that's a perfect opportunity to fill up on Divine Love. The setting couldn't be more ideal, so make the most of that time! Feel all that glowing deliciousness ooze down throughout your whole body, and imagine it's gently nudging any energy within you that is *not* love down, down, down . . . and then imagine that not-love energy slipping right out the bottom of your feet and swirling down the drain.

To live a life of authentic Juicy Joy, you must get very good at receiving love and filling up with love. Regularly working with these JuicyFeels will train your filter for that. You can receive love two ways, but you can only give it one way. As a human, you cannot give Divine Love, so there's no point in beating yourself up about that. World Love is the best you can do, and it's all that's expected of you. But when you are free and generous with your World Love, you are loving the divine within everything—and that is exactly what the divine most wants you to do.

~☙☙~

STEP THREE

JUDGMENT-FLIPPING

An important piece to becoming authentic is admitting that you're full of crap. Most people don't balk at that as much as you'd think they might. We all know, on some deep level, that we're full of crap. I certainly am, and I've spent decades purposefully working to eradicate that situation.

We all started out gloriously authentic, but our authenticity was soon buried under a barrage of judgments and fears about being judged. Judgment-Flipping is the skill we use in Juicy Joy training to examine and diffuse the power of judgments so that our true selves can shine forth unimpeded.

Over and over throughout our lives we've absorbed the message, implicitly and explicitly, that "image is everything," and "you don't get a second chance to make a first impression." As my friend who works in sales for a large publishing company quips, "Anybody who says you can't judge a book by its cover never tried to sell one." The cover is *all* we judge by! And all of us want our covers to be the shiniest, most impressive covers we can manage to project. But where does that really leave us in terms of self-love and genuine connection with our fellow humans?

Our inauthentic tendencies are often woven so deeply into the fiber of our beings that we have no idea they're even there. People-pleasing is an all-too-common and insidious addiction in our world, and I will forever be a recovering addict in that regard.

My Superhero Power

I grew up with the belief that I had to constantly twist myself into contortions in order to get love. I became a world-class eggshell walker . . . a skilled chameleon, so eager to please that I developed the superhero ability to intuit exactly what someone wanted from me and shape-shift instantly to transform myself into whatever would most delight the person in front of me—whether it was a friend, lover, boss, co-worker, or the deli clerk making my sandwich. Sounds like a handy talent to have, doesn't it?

Ironically, this "gift" of mine was the very thing that made genuine connection with others impossible for me. Deep connection was what I craved, but without any concrete sense of who I authentically was at my core, there was nothing there for anyone to connect *with,* and there was no way for me to comfortably enjoy the affection or attention I got from people, because deep down I always knew that it was contingent on my keeping up whatever mask I had spontaneously crafted in order to get that particular flavor of love in the first place.

This wasn't conscious effort on my part; it was completely automatic and unconscious, so it took full dedication to my Juicy Joy practices for me to finally successfully rid myself of the myriad masks I'd accumulated over all those years. The line that always tugged at me most in that beautiful Oriah poem was: "I want to know if you can disappoint another to be true to yourself." For most of my life, the answer was a clear-cut "no."

People-pleasers have a reputation as being super-giving, super-caring, super-loving types, right? We're not. That's just the illusion we project. The truth is that people-pleasers are the most selfish SOBs out there. Everything they do is motivated by a need to make

you *like* them. Because your attention, your admiration, is what sustains them—it's their lifeline, like blood to a vampire. They're going to do anything they can to suck it out of you.

I struggled with my people-pleasing addiction until the day I finally, after an excruciatingly long learning curve, locked into the deep *knowing* that I am whole and complete whether anyone approves of me or not. That may sound terribly mundane to you if you've never been afflicted with a people-pleasing addiction, but I can assure you it was monumental for me. My whole world opened up from there.

Judger and Judged

At the root of all people-pleasing tendencies, and most in-authentic tendencies in general, is a fear of being judged. Many of us grew up with some degree of a fear of abandonment from being found unlovable if we were judged and came up short. And we all judge *ourselves* to varying extents. If you don't think you judge yourself, it probably just means that you have a judgment about judging yourself.

If you're sensitive to the criticism of others, consider this: the extent to which you feel hurt by anyone's judgment of you is directly proportional to the degree to which you are already subconsciously judging that trait in yourself. (You might want to read that again.)

If I called you a jerk, you might feel insulted because most of us have a fear, deep down, that we have the capacity to be jerks. But if I called you a rhinoceros, you'd probably just think I was nuts and shrug it off. You know you're not a rhinoceros, so there's no way I can insult you with that—unless you have a big nose or a big butt that you're sensitive about, in which case your own self-judgment would cause you to feel insulted.

It's time to identify and deflate the judgments you make about yourself as well as those you make about others. Carl Jung was a brilliant psychotherapist who pointed out that we all have a

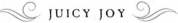

bunch of aspects of ourselves that we like to tuck away and hide. He named this group of aspects the "shadow self." Why would we hide all these perfectly natural bits of our humanness? Because these are the bits that we fear will be judged and held up as proof of our unlovableness.

The problem with hiding aspects of our authentic selves is that we can never really get rid of any part of us. Remember learning in science class that energy can neither be created nor destroyed? Well, we are energy. All of our feelings, emotions, and beliefs are energy. When we resist a particular aspect of ourselves (by repressing it and thereby making it part of our shadow), we are unconsciously feeding that very trait attention with our attempts to hide and deny it. Attention gives energy strength, so this kind of repression causes the resisted trait to magnify in our energy field.

The way this magnification typically shows up is that we become ubersensitive to this trait, but since we've repressed it in ourselves, we only notice it in other people. According to Jung, the judgments we make about others are based upon the judgments we subconsciously hold about ourselves. That is, the people who are the most harshly critical of others are actually the ones who are the most critical and judgmental of themselves, even if they outwardly appear to be overly confident.

The juicy-fabulous author Anaïs Nin puts it in more lyrical terms: "You do not see things as they are; you see them as you are." We've all witnessed examples of this. The gay-bashing politician who turns out to be homosexual himself. The wife beater who is always complaining about how unfairly he's treated by "the system" or by his employer. Debbie Ford, a brilliant teacher of shadow work, has a neat little pointing trick: she says that when you are pointing your finger at someone in judgment, you should check out who the other three fingers on that hand are pointing to.

Flip Those Judgments

Let's stretch a bit beyond this basic understanding of Jung's shadow theory. What if every judgment we make is a cause for

celebration because it has a valuable message for us? Your strong feelings are always gifts from the all-knowing Universe that adores you! On a conscious level, you may only register the thought that you dislike a particular trait in someone. But the discomfort you feel is actually a message from your subconscious alerting you to the very trait that is out of balance for *you*. The energy that fuels your judgment is the energy you are subconsciously storing in relationship to your own denial of that trait.

It's the Universe's way of showing you where you need to get in balance in order to move forward in your own life. Human traits are neither good nor bad when we accept them and balance them within ourselves. Any trait you harshly judge in another is a trait you are resisting, denying, and repressing in yourself. In order to live authentically, you'll need to dig it up and figure out how to own it in a healthy way.

Every human trait we deem negative has a perfectly acceptable flip, usually in its scaled-back version. For instance, if you notice rude people everywhere you go, and it disgusts you—you just abhor rudeness—you're likely to be someone who feels you are never rude, ever. So Jung's shadow stuff makes no sense to you. You're positive that you do not possess that trait you're seeing in others.

But the fact that it bothers you so much means your wiser self is trying to tell you something. It's telling you that your harsh judgment of this trait has knocked it out of balance for you. We are all made of the same source energy, and we all have *all of it* within us. The Universe wants you to stop resisting that fact. Your resistance is what is causing the uncomfortable feeling of judgment.

To find the healthy flip, see if you can identify a positive aspect of the trait you're judging by scaling it back. A scaled-back version of rudeness might simply be the ability to honor and express one's needs in a way that demands they be met. That's the healthy balance you're looking for. It only got out of whack for you because of some belief in your filter that made you start judging rudeness so harshly.

In this example, the person who hated rudeness has probably denied ownership of that trait to such a degree that she's being held back in life by not being clear enough about her own needs and wants, and not being direct enough to get them met. Her judgment of the trait sets up an internal struggle within her because she's unknowingly strangling even its healthier forms of expression. This would create a subconscious envy of the person who is abundantly forthright about his needs and is successful at having them met by others. The Universe might put increasingly rude people in her path until she got the message to balance this trait in herself.

A Juicy Joy student once asked, "Why can't the Universe just put people with the healthy version of the trait in our path so we could learn the balance from them?" That would be nicer, wouldn't it? But here's the thing. We are co-creators of our reality, and sometimes the best thing the Universe can do for us is show us what we've been creating. The degree to which our shadow aspects show up in unpleasant extremes in the people around us is the exact degree to which we've been judging those traits in ourselves.

Our feelings are what create our physical reality, remember? The Law of Attraction is a vibrational law, drawing to us whatever is a match to our vibration. So the rudeness hater will encounter despicable displays of rudeness because she finds the denied rudeness within her so despicable.

In the earlier example of the gay-bashing politician, isn't it likely that on some subconscious level, he'd be envious of homosexual lovers who were courageous enough to openly express their joyful unions? And wouldn't the wife beater (who fears he doesn't have enough control over his life and therefore exerts inappropriate force over another's) be jealous of "the system" that, from his perspective, seems to possess ultimate control? Can you see how getting their own traits in balance would help them release their judgments of others? And of themselves?

This is just one of the many reasons authentic self-love is so critical to our Juicy Joy. Every aspect of ourselves that we are

denying and refusing to love is routinely delivering unpleasant people and situations to us. So how do we stop the cycle of judgment? We correct it with Judgment-Flipping. We get underneath the judgment to figure out its message, and then we thank it and love it, thereby diffusing it of its negative power. Clearing up your judgments of yourself and others will have blissful ripple effects you can't even yet imagine!

One of My Judgment-Flipping Aha! Moments

I am exceptionally blessed to have many close friends who happen to be coaches, psychics, therapists, and self-dev rock stars. So they speak my language. Several years ago I was confiding in one such friend about an issue I was having with my then husband, Greg. Greg is a wonderful man, but he had a habit I couldn't stand—I called it "the tone." It felt to me like whenever something didn't go his way, he'd get this snarl in his lip and speak to me or the kids as though he were utterly disgusted with us.

My wise friend pointed out that I was judging Greg for his tone, and coached me to look for the feeling under the judgment. My immediate response was, "I hate that he doesn't have any concern for how his behavior might affect anyone else. It's selfish and insensitive."

She smiled. "Uh-huh. And just before you brought up Greg, what were you telling me?"

Oh. Oh, right. Lightbulb moment. I had been despairing to her over how torn and guilty I felt about spending more and more time away from my family. For most of my children's lives, my world had revolved around theirs, and I had neatly fit my author job into the hours they were at school. Now, for the first time, my work was leaking substantially over into hours I normally spent with them or volunteering in their classes, planning their events, and generally being available to them.

Just beneath the level of my conscious awareness, I was terrified that granting myself the "me" time I needed for my new career was selfish and insensitive. Owning "selfish and insensitive" was unbearable to me. Therefore, I attracted it outside of myself so I could point my judging finger at someone else.

Greg's "tone" was a message for me. I needed to see that I was jealous of my husband because he was able to easily grant himself freedoms that I was struggling to feel deserving of for myself. His "tone," in its healthy, scaled-back version, was simply a voice that said, "My needs in this family matter, too. Sometimes I'm going to put myself first."

Once I fully absorbed this message and got to work balancing out my own self-judgment, "the tone" almost completely disappeared. And that wasn't the only benefit. I realized that I'd been letting my irrational guilt over giving up my crown as Super Mom of the World throw a soggy wet blanket over my emerging excitement about my new career direction. I started enjoying my work more than ever, and it became clear that "the tone" had done me a fabulous favor!

I know this gets tricky, so let's recap: There was an aspect of me that I wasn't owning, called "I Want to Do Whatever I Want Without Worrying about How It Might Affect Anyone Else." It was a very real aspect of me that I had buried, because I judged it as being icky. Since I was judging and denying it in myself, it showed up outside of me. The energy that fueled my judgment of Greg was the energy of my own repressed self-judgment. My repression of that part of me had made it vibrationally active for me—therefore, I had attracted it via another person.

Another way to look at it is: The Universe that adores me wanted me to own and balance that aspect of myself so it generously gave me a kick in the pants via a "tone" from my husband. It may have previously given me scads of more subtle signs that I'd missed. And it would have given me more egregious signs if I'd been judging myself more egregiously.

Our judgments about ourselves keep us from feeling Juicy-Joyful self-love. Usually, the parts of us we've buried are carrying a lot of energetic weight even if we are completely unaware of them on a conscious level. Becoming aware of them so that we can balance and accept them releases that weight.

It was uncomfortable for me to admit that there's a part of me that wants to put myself before my kids. But now that I've dragged it out into the light, it's no big deal. I can own it, thank it for its self-loving intention, and balance it with my absolute devotion to those two sweetie pies I'd lay down my life for. Instead of hating it and letting it gnaw away at me from its festering hideout in my subconscious, I now welcome it as a perfectly natural and manageable piece of the glorious, perfect package that is me.

NakedWriting: What Bugs the Hell Out of You?

In your Juicy Joy journal, make a list of everything that bugs you about other people. It could have fifty people on it, or it could be mostly about one particular person who bugs you in many, many ways. Focus on all those irritants, and don't skimp.

Next, make a list of everything that bugs you about *you*. You did a similar exercise for the last step, but resist the urge to think back on it. Really think about what you judge most harshly about yourself.

Look at your lists now. Are there any traits that appear on both lists? Can you detect any instances where you're judging others in ways that are similar to the ways you're judging yourself? If you see similarities, jot them down. They represent the most basic application of Jungian shadow work.

Look into your past and see if you find any clues as to where the harsh judgment of this trait may have originated. From your now-broader, wiser perspective, does the judgment really seem warranted, or is it just an old habit? Can you find a way to accept this perfectly natural aspect of your humanness? Can you feel how accepting this trait in yourself automatically makes you more accepting of others who display it, even if they are displaying it in an amplified way you don't like?

Now look at the judgments you make about other people that you *don't* see in yourself. Every one of those judgments has a message for you. It's not as simple as, "I think you're stupid, so *I* must really be stupid." If you're judging someone for being stupid, it means you're hating and denying the perfectly natural part of you that doesn't always know everything you wish you knew. Acknowledging and making peace with that part of you will not only balance your judgment of yourself, but it will soften your judgment of others, too—and consequently, you'll encounter stupidity less often. Once you've acknowledged and released the judgment, the Universe can stop clobbering you with the message.

A common dynamic I often see in my trainings is one where a mom is having a difficult time with her teenage daughter. Typically, the mother is judging the daughter for what she perceives as a haughty, rebellious sense of entitlement. Since it's so common for moms to lose themselves in the course of their parenting journeys, they're naturally triggered by seeing an emerging adult—especially a daughter—enthusiastically declaring her authentic self to the world and claiming her right to be whatever she wants to be. Once these moms examine the judgment and see that it's really about their own repressed desires to feel more "entitled" and self-honoring, they can appreciate and be inspired by their daughters, which smoothes out much of the conflict between them.

See if you can find the acceptable flip to some of your judgments of others by scaling the attribute back to a healthier version. Are there any instances where the annoying trait, scaled back to a positive version, is a trait you could be jealous of? A trait that the Universe might be wanting to alert you to? (If the answers aren't clear to you, look back at the example I gave with Greg's "tone.") Ask yourself, "Why does this bother me? What accusation-feeling underlies this judgment? What does this imply about the person?" This is important, so spend some time with it. Write your insights in your Juicy Joy journal.

NakedWriting: Let's Get Naked with Our Self-Judgments

Set a clear intention to bring up parts of yourself that you've been suppressing, and just decide that for the next few moments you will drop any resistance you might be feeling about this kind of self-inquiry. You actually *want* to bring up unflattering and negative stuff here, because you need to root up all those judgments about yourself that you don't even know you're making. Finding an unflattering trait in this exercise doesn't mean that it's *true*. It just means that it's a belief you've been holding.

I'm going to give you a prompt, and I want you to keep repeating it, allowing whatever comes after it to just flow out onto the paper. Do this for at least ten minutes. More would be good.

Write the words, *If you really knew me, you'd know* . . . and see what comes after those words. Repeat this until you feel there's nothing left.

Did you find some surprises? Look at the judgments you make about yourself. Even if some of them seem to be true, they're really just beliefs you've been storing in your filter. If you have a lot of seeming "evidence" in your life to support these beliefs, consider that the only thing this proves is that you *have* the belief. We make the mistake of thinking that the evidence proves the belief is true, when in reality we created these circumstances *because* the belief was there.

Beliefs are just energy. Energy can neither be created nor destroyed, but energy changes form all the time. You have the power, right now, to shift the energy of these beliefs by consciously embracing and balancing the judgments you hold about yourself.

Farther Down the Rabbit Hole

I hope you're feeling up to speed on this rather large concept, because I'm going to take it a step further. Not only will your self-judgments show up outside of you in unpleasant ways, but they will also cause you to unconsciously reinforce them with your own behavior and actions. In the same way that your beliefs about the world create the world you experience, your beliefs about yourself will create circumstances wherein you do and say things in accordance with those beliefs. Identifying negative self-judgments for healing is trickier in these cases because instead of seeing evidence of your judging patterns outside of you, you have to look for the evidence in your own behavior.

Here's an example: During one of those phases when I was beating myself up about neglecting my family in favor of my work, my son, Tucker, was invited to the Bar Mitzvah of two good friends of his, twins. It was Tuck's first Bar Mitzvah, and he was excited. The invitation was up on the fridge, and he had a stylin' new outfit to wear. But since the boys had gone to different middle schools, Tuck wasn't around anyone who was talking about the upcoming event, nor was he mature enough to manage his own calendar.

We missed it. No excuse. I was simply preoccupied with preparations for an upcoming retreat and didn't realize the date had passed until several days later. It was completely out of character for me, and I was utterly devastated when we discovered it. Tuck was sweet because that's his nature, but naturally, he was disappointed.

It would have been easy to view this situation as evidence that I truly had become an awful mom, which would have further cemented the harmful belief in my filter. Thankfully, I was able to instead recognize that I had fallen into the trap of allowing an insidious belief to create a situation to support it. I knew that I never would have let Tuck miss such a special event before the recent "bad mom" judgment had worked its way into my filter.

That experience was the wake-up call that made me finally pull the belief out and examine it so that I could balance it for good. I listed all the ways I believed I was being a bad mom and neglecting my kids. I came to understand that my irrational need to be a perfect mother had caused me to disown the completely natural parts of me that weren't so perfect in that department. Anything that we disown in ourselves becomes the target for our harshest judgments—oftentimes of others, but in this case, I'd turned the judgment on myself.

Through honest introspection, I came to see all the ways in which I was actually becoming a better and better mom. My personal-development career, though it took up much of my time, had given me innumerable skills for guiding my kids and supporting them, and being an ever-better example for them to follow.

They were becoming more independent as a result of my work schedule. By sincerely apologizing to Tuck about failing to get him to the Bar Mitzvah, I was able to model how to deal with making a mistake.

I believe that my deliberate attention to balancing that "bad mom" judgment in my filter was the reason the ensuing events went so smoothly. I called the mother of the Bar Mitzvah boys, a friend I had shared room-mom duties with for many years, to apologize, and she could not have been more understanding. It turned out she had recently done the same thing, causing her boys to miss another friend's Bar Mitzvah! Tuck and I decided to throw a karaoke pool party in honor of his friends' milestone. The kids got to continue their celebrating, and we all had a fabulous time. 'Cause I rock as a mom.

The judgments we hold about ourselves—both conscious and unconscious—have an enormous impact on our actions and what we create in our lives. In the words of the immortal Louise Hay, "Your thoughts and beliefs of the past have created this moment, and all the moments up to this moment. What you are now choosing to believe and think and say will create the next moment and the next day and the next month and the next year."

The Only Way Out Is Through

The better we get at recognizing and blessing the complete spectrum of traits, emotions, and attributes that comprise our full authentic selves, the closer we'll be to our Juicy Joy. But as you've probably noticed, digging up all this dirt on ourselves is no picnic. We're almost done, but we're going to do one more NakedWriting exercise, now that you're all loosened up with the previous ones. It isn't exactly fun. Rest assured that plenty of fun is coming up in future steps, but we'll only be able to fully experience that joy after we've gone through this last bit of muck.

Because I love you and I feel for you in this part of your journey, I'm going to give you a treat first. My friend Libba Bray, who is arguably today's very hottest author of young-adult novels and a regular on the *New York Times* bestsellers list, goes through this painful yet liberating process of turning herself inside out every time she writes a new book. She writes fiction, but the resistance to vulnerability she encounters is no different from the kind I'm asking you to overcome in your NakedWriting. In a blog post (**http://libba-bray.livejournal.com/61178.html**), Libba says:

> One of the things that continues to surprise me about the writing life is how bloody impossible it can seem at times. I always feel that somehow I should have figured out how this whole thing works, but I swear that every single book is like learning how to write all over again. It's learning not to break and run when you start dredging up those ghosts of the subconscious, those deep-down scary things that we do our best in our everyday lives to ignore. I've written five books now, and I know this is part of the process, and yet I am always surprised, dismayed, and panicked to find myself in this spot. I'm telling you this happens EVERY SINGLE FRIGGIN' TIME.
>
> Usually, I get a sense that this is about to happen because I become agitated and completely avoidant. I will whimper and pace the way dogs do before a bad storm. There will be a few days, maybe a week or two, sometimes even a month, in which the writing feels terribly stilted. False. Awful. The equivalent of small talk at a party where you don't know anybody and you can't leave yet because somebody else is driving, and so you just have to keep standing in the corner holding on to your sweating seltzer glass saying, "Really? How interesting. I did not know that about elephants."
>
> I hate this part. Hate it. These are the days when I come home with the comic book dark cloud scribbles over my head, and when my husband asks me how the writing's going, I sigh and press my head against my palms and moan, "Terrible. I can't figure this thing out. I don't

know anything about writing books. You have to tell them I don't know how to write books. The last five books were a fluke, and now it's over. Over, I tell you. I'm so sorry. I tried. I have to go watch *The Simpsons* now."

When I've done school and library visits and people have asked me how I deal with writer's block, I usually say that I do a free write. That the act of confession on paper helps me to get out of my own way.

So what would I tell you if I could? I would tell you that this book scares me. That on some level, it feels too big, too unwieldy, too . . . much. Like I'm a very small knight in ill-fitting armor dragging an untested sword, and I'm staring up at a gigantic, multi-headed, fire-breathing dragon who's working a good smirk. (Those dragons, big on the smirk, which, if you ask me, is just overkill. I mean, dudes, you've already got flight and fire. Give the snark a rest.) These fears are, I'm sure, pretty universal. But in the moment, they feel so very personal.

This is the magic/curse of writing: That in crafting your fiction, you leave yourself open to sudden moments of unguarded truth, and you have to be willing to tolerate that again and again. You have to keep raising your sword and charging, even knowing you could retreat scorched and missing a limb. You have to keep doing it even when you don't want to. Especially when you don't want to.

The act of confession on paper *will* get you out of your own way, whether you're trying to create a novel or trying to create a more authentic and self-loving life for yourself.

You have to keep doing it, even when you don't want to. Especially when you don't want to. Suck it up, my juicy love. Raise your sword and forge onward.

NakedWriting: The Muck

In your Juicy Joy Journal, armed with your insights from all the exercises you've just done, being as raw and naked and vulnerable as possible, answer these questions:

- What lies are you telling yourself, right now, about your life?

- What lies are you telling others?

- What is your payoff for lying to others?

- What is your payoff for lying to yourself?

- What is your deepest fear about yourself?

- What is your worst anxiety?

- What are your worst beliefs about yourself?

Take some time to let the answers to those questions settle fully into your consciousness.

Ready to go another round? I'm going to ask you some more questions, but I want you to feel the answers. Don't rummage around in your head—feel around in your gut. Take longer with these responses, and you may not repeat any of the answers you gave above, even though the questions are similar, and even if you believe your first answer was deep. Dig deeper. Those were your head-answers and you want to access your heart-answers.

Don't try to be spiritual or noble. If you must try to be anything, try to be vulnerable, self-incriminating. Fetter out the memories that embarrass or shame you the most. This will yield the best result.

- How have you most significantly hurt another?

- How have you most significantly hurt yourself?

- When have you been the most manipulative?

- When have you been the most critical of yourself?

- When have you been the most critical of another?

- When have you apologized for who you are?
- When have you tried the hardest to hide who you really are?
- When have you sold yourself out?
- When have you been most abusive?
- When have you been most disrespectful?
- When have you been the most self-destructive?
- What do you most regret?
- What is your worst habit?
- What are you most ashamed of?

Be sure to satiate all these questions. If tears come, that's wonderful! Invite sadness. Invite shame. Invite anger, and be grateful for all of it. This is a beautiful process! Whatever resistance you feel around these questions is an indication that you're digging up some stuck energy. Rejoice in that! We all have these buried bits, so don't judge yourself for them—feel them, embrace them, allow them to surface. Love yourself for being brave enough to uproot all these pieces of you. Each one has helped you to grow and evolve. Lay them on the table and shower them with awe and gratitude and affection! Only when you can fully embrace all of these murky aspects will you be freed from their hold!

JuicyFeel to Heal Self-Judgments

We're going to heal all of these judgments now with a tremendously powerful JuicyFeel meditation.

— Once you've moved your body and gotten into alpha state, I want you to imagine yourself standing in front of a large cauldron. In this cauldron is every single unflattering bit of you that you've dug up with these exercises.

— Stir all these negative aspects together and feel how dense and heavy they are. What would it take for you to forgive yourself of these crimes and balance these judgments you hold against yourself and others? Do you feel that they've loosened up a bit already, simply from your acknowledgment of them?

— Now pretend that this is a scene in a movie and you're the lead character. The theater is full of people who have just watched the movie of your entire life up to this point, and it's a magical movie theater where they were able to telepathically experience every thought you've had along the way as well. The audience, naturally, is made of the same source energy you are made of— the same source energy all people everywhere are made of. They know that everything in the cauldron belongs to them as much as it belongs to you. Even if something in the cauldron is especially painful for you, understand that every person watching—along with every person on the planet—has some kind of similar secret shame they're reluctant to feel.

— The moviegoers are powerfully rooting for you, the main character up there stirring your cauldron of regrets, remorse, and hurtful memories—your cauldron that is so similar to each of theirs. They're projecting their hopes and dreams onto you. You are their hero. Don't you love watching a movie when you deeply relate to the main character? Don't you always want what's best for him, even if he's made some mistakes during the course of the film?

— As you stir, an energetic aspect of you floats up out of your body and hovers near the top of the screen. It's your God-self, the very wisest, purest, most divine part of you. What is this God-aspect feeling toward you? Is it angry about what's in the cauldron? Is it judging you at all? Or is it compassionate? Understanding? Maybe it's nodding proudly, acknowledging that you chose a path that involved some tough twists and turns, but here you are—owning every bit of it, not denying anything, courageously taking responsibility for the totality of your journey thus far. The moviegoers are on the edge of their seats.

— Main-Character-You looks up at the radiantly glowing God-You with gratitude and awe at its perfection. God-You smiles, then gracefully dives directly down into the cauldron, disappearing into its swirling contents!

— The audience gasps! In a flash of light, the viscous mixture becomes as clean and smooth and sparkling as the Divine Love you imagined in the Filter-Fixing Step. It's blindingly white and twinkling with juicy goodness. All of those aspects of you are still in there, but they're now merged with the higher understanding that every one of them had a meaningful purpose and place in your life. Blended with the forgiveness energy of your own all-powerful divinity, your self-judgments have transmuted into gorgeous, bubbly, iridescent acceptance and self-love. The audience goes wild, leaping from their seats to clap and cheer for you.

— Feel the exquisite release as the heaviness you've been carrying slides away. You are now forever free of that dense burden! Spread your arms, throw your head back, and twirl. Let out a rich, throaty laugh. Wiggle your hips and do a victory dance around the cauldron. Whip out a crazy straw and suck up the contents. Fill yourself with scrumptious, nourishing, decadent self-love. Feel lighter and freer with every slurp.

You're on the Self-Love Fast Track!

Transmuting your self-judgments into self-love doesn't mean that you won't have the incentive to make further changes in yourself toward ever-greater degrees of Juicy Joy. Of course you will continue to grow and evolve, but you will do it much more speedily and effectively now! Genuine change can only happen when you are first accepting and loving every part of you.

If you try to change anything from a position of "I hate this aspect of me," you will gain nothing from the change. If you hate your nose and get a nose job so you have a perfect one, it will only be a matter of time before you hate something else about yourself. Your nose wasn't the problem; hating yourself was.

Conversely, when you accept and love all of who you are, making changes is fun! You can be as creative and daring as you please. You know that you are fantastic now and you will continue to be fantastic, and that makes it exciting to change and grow.

Is it hard to believe that you've accomplished such a substantial shift within yourself by simply imagining it? Remember the power of deep pretending. In the energetic part of you where your beliefs reside, there is no difference between what happens in the physical world and what happens in your imagination, so long as you're vividly *feeling* it. But maybe you want a little proof that you've done some genuine shifting. Try the following JuicyFeel.

JuicyFeel: Prove It

— Pick someone from the list you made earlier of people you judge and imagine this person standing in front of you.

— Knowing that you're both made of the same source energy, acknowledge that this person has a soul's path that has overlapped with your own soul's path in some way that was unpleasant to you but afforded you a growth opportunity.

— In your imagination, look deeply into this person's eyes and say, "I honor your path."

— If it feels really good, go ahead and do it with everyone on that list. Then wrap your arms around *yourself* and say, "I honor your path."

Do you think you would have been able to do this exercise if it had been the first thing in this chapter? Do you believe now that you've shifted your energy in mysteriously powerful and wonderful ways?

Sameness of Bearing

Releasing judgments of yourself and others is a magical authenticity enhancer. One of the qualities Buddhists strive for on the path to enlightenment is called "sameness of being," or "sameness of bearing." It means being exactly who you authentically are, no matter who you are interacting with. The examples given are usually in reference to how we address those we perceive to be in positions of power above us or beneath us. For example, one who practices sameness of bearing would speak to the president of his company in exactly the same manner he spoke to the janitor of the building he worked in.

But my "Aha!" moment with this principle several years ago went beyond mere power-positioning. I had been happily giving successful out-of-town personal-development workshops as part of my travels to schools across the country, but had not yet attempted that genre in my hometown. When I did finally decide to offer a workshop at a local metaphysical center, I sent out an e-mail inviting everyone I knew. I thought of it as a bit of a coming-out with my new career direction, away from mainstream publishing and into the more spiritual and metaphysical realm I'd been privately passionate about for so long.

I bombed horrifically. It was by far the worst workshop I ever led, and that was entirely due to my own internal, last-minute freak-out. I hadn't anticipated it happening, but when I looked at my audience and saw my neighbors who knew me one way, intermingled with the parents of my kids' friends who knew me another way, intermingled with my very metaphysically minded friends who knew a completely different side of me . . . I froze. My brain literally could not sort out who I was supposed to be in that moment. I suddenly became uberaware that many of these people had come merely to support me and were not actually interested in my subject matter. That shouldn't have made any difference, but it did.

It was humbling to realize the extent to which I still routinely contorted myself to fit what I imagined to be people's expectations of me. And like all painfully uncomfortable experiences, it provided a power boost for my growth in that area. The Buddhist "sameness of bearing" principle took center stage in my self-dev routine after that, and it's still a pivotal piece of my consciousness practice. Thank you, Universe, for that awful experience.

It's Nothing Personal

To be your most authentic self, you must get over your habits of worrying about what people think of you and taking things that other people say or do personally. I highly recommend the books of don Miguel Ruiz. One of his life-transforming Four Agreements is: *Don't take anything personally.*

Appreciation is the opposite of taking something personally. You can't appreciate something and judge it negatively at the same time. The following JuicyFeel will cement your new nonjudgmental ways into your filter. Practice it so that you can pull it out and apply it in situations that might normally inspire judgment. It's great to slip into when you're entering a work or social situation where you don't feel completely comfortable, or when you sense that there could be some kind of antagonism toward you—with difficult family members or a tense office environment, for example. You'll want to have this one on audio to carry around with you.

JuicyFeel: All Is Well in the Deep Blue Sea

— Go through your processes of moving and pleasurably reaching alpha state.

— Fill up with Divine Love.

— Imagine that you are a deep-sea diver. You are completely safe in your diver gear and you love this hobby of yours. You are passionate about exploring marine life and coral. You relish the peaceful, no-sound zone of the undersea world, so rich with things to discover and appreciate.

— If the thought of this feels at all scary to you, take whatever imaginary precautions you need to invent to let you feel that this experience is indisputably safe in every way. Put up an imaginary force field around you, or put yourself in a clear bubble that is completely impenetrable. This is your imagination, so make sure that you are supremely protected and relaxed.

— Notice all the beautiful colors, all the interesting creatures. Some fish are charming and adorable, and others are intimidating looking, with long pointy teeth and bug eyes, but you welcome them all with equal fascination and curiosity.

— You can wonder how a fish got that way, or you can mentally compare its features with other fish you've seen. But there's no reason to fear or feel threatened by any of them. You love and appreciate them all equally, because observing fascinating creatures and scenery is what you've come down here to do. Some might even present obstacles for you, but that's just an exciting adventure to the deep-sea diver.

— Keep saying to yourself, "How interesting!" about the lovely and graceful creatures, about the menacing and shocking ones. You're so, so safe and joyful, floating in your undersea world.

If you practice this little JuicyFeel for just a few minutes each day, you'll be able to start accessing that feeling when you need it in your life. The grouchy landlord, the demeaning boss, the nagging friend, the insulting parent—they all simply become interesting fishies! They're all on their own paths and you're on yours, and you can appreciate all the fascinating perspectives they allow you to contemplate.

Appreciation cancels judgment. And freeing yourself from judgment keeps you in vibrational alignment with everything you want to bring into your life.

Judgment-Flipping in a Juicy Nutshell

Are you feeling a bit emotionally Roto-Rootered? See what I meant about clearing out those emotional catacombs? Most people walk around storing so many horrible opinions about themselves and others, and they have no idea how powerfully those judgments are keeping their dreams and their joy perpetually out of reach. You've taken some dramatic steps toward releasing those shackles, and you're probably feeling much lighter already.

Pay attention to the circumstances of your life now, and observe how infrequently you experience the people and situations that used to cause you the most grief. The degree to which you've released the energetic force that was pulling their unpleasantness to you (your judgments) is the precise degree to which they'll disappear from your reality. Staying aware of that fact should help you to continue deliberately releasing any remnants of judgment that remain.

If you find any of those lingering remnants especially difficult to dismantle, they're probably embedded in repetitive stories you've been telling yourself throughout your lifetime. These stories tend to give judgments and limiting beliefs extra sticking power, so we're going to examine that phenomenon in the next chapter, and we'll go through some processes to rewrite any stories that could potentially tempt your limitations and judgments to return.

Before we start Story-Stripping, enjoy this final Judgment-Flipping JuicyFeel.

JuicyFeel to Release Judgment of Everything

— Move pleasurably and go to alpha state.

— Imagine yourself into the starting position for the "You on Top of the World" JuicyFeel you learned in the Emotion-Mixing Step.

— Instead of going into your giving-and-receiving routine, lie your body down on the world, wrapping your arms and legs around the earth the way koalas wrap themselves around trees.

— Rest your cheek against the world, and feel all its busy, diverse energies pulsing beneath you.

— Pour love from your heart directly into this amazing, incomprehensibly exciting world. So many intriguing possibilities; so many opportunities and unknown treasures.

— Feel the world sending love back into your heart—World Love, of course, with all its colors and spices and chunkiness and wonder.

— Allow the love to flow back and forth between you and the world in a gentle, undulating rhythm.

— Then feel another love wrapping itself around you from behind, like a blanket. It's Divine Love—pristine perfection, blanketing you as it blankets the whole Earth.

— Allow the Divine Love to seep into your being, filling every cell with its rich magnificence. You are fully encompassed in love.

This is a really nice way to fall asleep.

STEP FOUR

STORY-STRIPPING

We all have stories that define us. They feel like "the truth" about our lives, but the truth is that there is no objective reality —we create our reality with our attention and where we place our focus. We rely on our stories to support our judgments and the other beliefs we carry around in our filters. But they're really nothing more than elaborately adorned versions of our beliefs—beliefs with lots of accessories. It's easy to point to our outer circumstances as "evidence" that these stories are true . . . but again I want you to consider that the only thing this "evidence" proves is that the beliefs exist. The beliefs created the situations.

Some of your stories are probably serving you. You might have a story about all the schooling and training you've done to become a leader in your field, and believing that story gives you confidence to follow your dreams with ever-bolder career moves. You might have a story about how you met your spouse that confirms your feeling that destiny brought you together, and that story might be contributing a sweet detail to your love for one another.

Yet you probably have some stories that are *not* serving you. Even though you've done great work so far to remove limiting beliefs from your filter and flip judgments you were holding about yourself and the world, there may be a few more stubborn beliefs that require extra attention. Usually these are the ones that are backed by stories.

Are You Stuck in the Spin Cycle?

Have you ever noticed a recurring theme in your love life, your work life, your friendships, or the way in which you approach your goals? Are there any patterns? (Hint: If there's an area of your life you're particularly dissatisfied with right now, chances are good that you can find some repetitive cycles in *that* area.)

Remember how much the Universe adores you? Remember how it's always guiding you along your particular life path that leads you to your greatest joy? Part of the loving Universe's job is to educate you. In the Emotion-Mixing Step, you learned how to blend your sadness and anger over the hardships in your life with some better-feeling emotions. Knowing that those hardships were there to teach you and help you evolve toward your Juicy Joy is what allowed you to do that. So if you detect a pattern in your life of similar recurring hardships, it can only mean one thing. There's something the Universe needs you to know, and you aren't *getting it* yet.

The Universe will not give up on you. It will give you the same opportunity to learn something a thousand times until you figure it out. And since the Universe loves you so much, it might up the ante on the lesson if you're really thick.

NakedWriting for Discovering Patterns

If most of your romantic relationships have ended in the same way, or for the same reasons, take a moment to write about that in your journal. Look at the jobs you've had, the friendships you've had, your past hobbies or interests. Jot down your thoughts about any patterns you see.

If you did detect some patterns, take a few moments to do NakedWriting in your journal using this prompt: *If the Universe were trying to tell me something, what would it be?* Don't use your head to answer the question. Stop thinking about it, and feel into it instead.

You only had to learn the capital of Nebraska once in elementary school to be forevermore excused from that particular geography lesson. In the same way, the Universe will be delighted to graduate you once you get the point. The moment you internalize what the Universe is trying to teach you, you won't have to experience that unpleasant story ever again.

What Are You Watering?

It feels like our stories are created outside of us, by the things that occur in our lives. But as we've already discussed, our beliefs create our circumstances, and everything that occurs is subject to many possible interpretations. So our stories are actually created by our beliefs and perceptions, and then fed and strengthened by the attention we've chosen to funnel into them.

Imagine right now that there's a faucet on your forehead, right at your third eye, with a garden-hose attachment on it. You send your attention out into the world through this hose. Everything that's in your life is a seed, the good and the bad. Whatever you're giving your attention to—those are the seeds you're watering. That's what's going to grow for you. Those are the seedlings that will sprout into stories if you water them enough.

If you've got a problem and you put a lot of focus and attention on *resisting* that problem, you're watering the hell out of that seed. Even if you eventually struggle through this particular issue, hating every second of it, and somehow wrangle it under control, you've watered the seeds of the *essence* of the problem, so just like weeds around it, more of the same kind of problem is going to keep popping up.

That's why people tend to keep repeating their stories by experiencing the same flavor of unhealthy relationship patterns, the same financial difficulties, the same health issues. Whenever you develop a strong negative feeling about an experience, and put a lot of resistance into experiencing it (as opposed to welcoming any natural emotions that arise and looking for the lesson), you strengthen the seemingly magnetic force that brought it to you in the first place.

What if the only thing stopping you from creating your ideal reality is your failure to conjure up an ideal "story seed" for yourself that you can believe in long enough to water it with the requisite amount of your attention?

You're reading this book because there's something you want to add to your life. You have a delicious story, perhaps only vaguely formed, that you want to live. To make room for that story, we need to clear out some old stories that no longer serve you and free up the energy they're storing.

No one likes to think of him- or herself as a victim, but many of us unwittingly cast ourselves as victims all the time in the way we choose to perceive the events of our lives. And calling an event a victim story doesn't mean it isn't true or that we're overdramatizing it—it's simply a story in which we feel that we were on the receiving end of something undesirable.

So nod your head if anything bad has ever happened to you. We've all felt victimized by the world at some point. You may have shifted your judgments and beliefs on a lot of your victim stories already, so as you go through the exercises in this chapter, just notice what authentically comes up for you. The more real you can be with your answers, the more fully you'll be able to discharge any unwelcome bits that might be lingering in your filter.

NakedWriting: It Totally Sucked

In your Juicy Joy journal, jot down the first answers that come to you in response to the following questions:

- How have you been most abused?

- How have you been most disrespected?

- When were you most misunderstood?

- When have you tolerated more than you should have?

- When have you stayed in unhealthy relationships?

- How have you been most significantly hurt or betrayed? It could be by your partner, parents, kids, a friend . . .

Look at all of the victim stories you wrote down, and find the one that stings the most. It might be the most recent, or it might be something that happened long ago. Put a star next to that one.

Now write out your starred victim story with the intention of being as whiny as possible. You really want to feel the victim role for this exercise—this is you at your petty worst. Be a drama queen or king. Convince your imaginary audience that you are a world-class victim. This is your private journey, so don't hold anything back.

How did it feel to tell the story from that angle? For some people, it's hugely liberating, because they've never let themselves indulge in the sadness around the event before. People who are too afraid of being a victim sometimes deprive themselves of feeling the deep sadness that needs to have the chance to flow through them in order to be released.

For some people, the opposite is true. If, in telling your story as a victim, you started to feel silly or embarrassed by the way you were complaining, it could mean that you just really don't have very strong victim feelings around this issue—but it could also be a sign that you've gotten a payoff for being a victim, and you've begun to identify yourself too closely with this story. If you feel like you can hear your voice in the story but don't really feel it in your gut, you may be hanging on to this story primarily out of habit.

The problem is that there are many ways in which our society rewards victims, and that can cause us, subconsciously, to identify with our victim stories more than we need to. Whatever we focus on is what we magnify in our lives, so the more focus we place on our victim stories, the more power we give them to hold us captive.

This phenomenon is especially common among people with persistent health issues. Once you identify yourself with a poor health condition, it can become difficult to ever move past that story. Often people get lots of attention, perks, and advantages from having a health crisis. As much as they might want to be "cured" on a conscious level, they remain subconsciously tied to their illness because they don't want to give up the perks that come with it. Unbeknownst to them, their story is keeping them sick.

No matter what your particular victim story is, can you recognize that there are two distinctly separate components to it? There is the event itself, which was simply a thing that occurred. And then there is your interpretation of the event. Can you see how your suffering was caused by the meaning that you ascribed to the event, rather than being caused by the event itself?

The meanings that we ascribe to things are determined by our filters. For example, pregnancy is an event. Perceived through one woman's filter, it's a cause for celebration. Perceived through another woman's filter, however, it's catastrophic. Same event, different filters. So considering that events have no meaning until we ascribe a meaning to them, you're going to write your victim story again from a very different perspective.

NakedWriting: Just the Facts, Ma'am

In your Juicy Joy Journal, take the same story you just wrote about, and this time write it from the perspective of a totally dry, unemotional newscaster. Just the facts describing the event; nothing more, nothing less. Same story, different perspective. To that end, a newscaster might drily report, "Rig blast causes ten-mile-wide oil spill in the Gulf. Details at 11." He's not going to say, "Holy crap, you're not gonna believe this but oil is gushing out into the ocean! It's killing marine life! It's polluting our water! It's going to destroy our ecosystem and compromise life on Earth as we know it! How could a thing like this happen? It's just devastating! *Ahhhh!*"

Write your story now, newscaster style. When you're done, think about how it felt to write it that way. Was it hard to stick to the unemotional facts?

One of my most brilliant teachers has been Byron Katie. In her landmark book *Loving What Is*, she goes through a process that starts with your victim story and asks the question, "Is it true?" to help people break through the illusion that the way they perceive the world is the "accurate" way. Once you've answered, "Yes, it's true," she asks: "Can you absolutely know that it's true?" The process goes on to dissect the original statement to the point where it's completely obvious that there is no objective truth to it.

How many times in your life have you felt absolutely positive that something was true, and it turned out otherwise? The divorce rate speaks to that fact, right? When you get married, aren't you absolutely positive that you'll be madly in love forever? And how could we ever truly know such a thing—not only about ourselves, but about another person as well? We cling to our convictions because they make us feel safe. But it's a false sense of security. Convictions freeze up our energy. They make us rigid and unable to flow with the ever-changing circumstances of our lives.

We all have the power to assign whatever meanings we choose to the events in our lives. When we don't know we have that power, we assign meanings unconsciously—and for most of us, that's not to our advantage.

NakedWriting: You Have the Answers

In your journal, I want you to write your victim story—that same story—one last time. This time, you're going to write it from the perspective of your own higher wisdom, that God-aspect of you. You need to assume that this event happened for your growth, for your highest good somehow. Even if it doesn't seem possible that this is true, see if you can find some glimmer of a hook to bend it that way. You don't have to believe it as you're writing it. Just pretend that your life depends on your finding a way to write it from that angle, even if it feels like pure bullshit.

How did it feel to write it this time? Do you feel any sense of loosening of the energy around this story? Does it feel a little freer or lighter or less constricting in your body to consider the possibility that you have something to be thankful for regarding this issue?

Would you *like* to be able to see it this way? If you'd like to but feel that you aren't able to, you need to ask yourself why. The only logical reason why you wouldn't just make the choice to adopt a different viewpoint is that you're getting some kind of payoff for staying stuck in the negative energy pattern. If you look closely at what the payoff might be, you can then weigh the pros and cons of holding this grudge against this particular situation or person. Maybe you'll decide that the payoff is worth it, and that's okay if you do. Recognizing that you're getting a payoff will at least help you to blend appreciation into resentment, which will begin to release the stuck energy there.

Radically Forgive

One of my favorite quotes attributed to that cheeky philosopher Albert Einstein is: "Insanity is doing the same thing over and over again and expecting different results." This is what hanging on to your story is like. If the story has always made you miserable, it always will. Hanging on to it is kind of insane. You have the ability to use your conscious attention to rewrite the stories that define you

In his beautiful book *Radical Forgiveness,* Colin Tipping talks about the powerful moment when you realize that whatever happened that now begs your forgiveness happened not *to* you, but *for* you. It happened so you could evolve, grow, or experience the contrast that would give your life more meaning and depth. He

says that when you can thank the person or circumstance you set out to forgive, that's when you know you've achieved radical forgiveness, which sets *you* free, not the recipient of the forgiveness. Forgiveness does not change the past, or condone any action. But it does free the forgiver, and allow for a joyful future.

A common soul-communication technique that I've encountered in different formats from many teachers is a practice I've nicknamed "Meet Me Upstairs." Although it can be used for any kind of message you want to send soul to soul, it works especially well for forgiveness and letting go of the stuck energy of conflict with someone. (The person does not need to be living for this to be extremely effective.)

JuicyFeel: Meet Me Upstairs

— Move, stretch, and get comfortable in alpha brain-wave state.

— Close your eyes and imagine your spirit leaving your body and floating up to a higher dimension.

— Picture the spirit of the person you want to address doing the same.

— Imagine your two souls meeting in this higher dimension, face-to-face.

— Say everything you want to say, and listen to what this person's soul has to say to you.

— Together, discuss what lessons each of you may have learned from one another. What good has come from your relationship?

— What aspects of your interactions have you been unwilling to acknowledge? Acknowledge them now.

— What beliefs do you need to release in order to move forward in love? Release them now.

— When it feels right, imagine your two souls hugging. If you're doing deep forgiveness work, you may need to go through the exercise many times before the hug feels genuine. Do it that many times.

I suggest that you revisit all the victim stories you recorded in your journal and repeat this chapter's exercises for each of them. It's the best way to release the stuck energy of stories from your past. Only when you bring them out into the light can you consciously rewire them.

Take a moment to fully recognize that you have the power to shift the energy within any story that holds you back. Your stories are made of energy, and energy changes form all the time. You can't squeeze it in your hands or put it in a bag. It's just energy, and we do have the ability to take charge and manage the energy that we embody.

JuicyFeel: Clean Slate

— After moving your body and settling into alpha, leisurely enjoy your whole Mirror You JuicyFeel.

— After Mirror You has stepped out of the mirror and into your body, look around your nature setting and see a lookout tower.

— As your ideal self, walk over to the lookout tower and climb the stairs.

— From this vantage point you can look down and see all the stories you've created that have been limiting you from reaching your highest potential. Beam at them proudly.

— Hold your hands to your heart and send love and blessings down to these stories for helping you to get to the perfect place where you now are. They've each served an essential purpose in your life path.

— Imagine a gentle breeze kicking up, and smile, knowing that the albatross aspects of your stories are made of ash.

— Watch as the breeze softly blows each story clean, forever erasing from your consciousness any parts that are no longer serving you.

— From the lookout tower you can see that releasing these limiting energies has opened up a whole field of receptive clean-slate energy for writing new stories to carry you forward.

— Relish the thought of creating these new stories. Rub your hands together in juicy anticipation!

Juicy Embodiment Practice: New Story!

Whenever you catch yourself getting caught up in one of your past stories, mentally say the word, "Story!" Your awareness will interrupt the energetic pull of the old story so that you can take conscious control. Vividly imagine the moment in the above Juicy-Feel when you rub your hands together. In real time, rub your actual hands together while focusing on the scrumptious new story you're creating to replace the old one. Feel the juice.

Get Into the Story-Free Zone

There is a narrow, exquisite space between your past stories and your future stories called "the now." The more you can train yourself to live in the now, the easier it will be for you to free yourself from the energetic tugs of your stories.

My 14-year-old son, Tucker, is my best teacher of staying in the now. I call him Present-Moment Man. He somehow manages to structure the vast majority of his present moments so that they're filled with the things he loves, and he becomes so deeply absorbed in these pursuits that it's impossible to pull him out.

I believe that present-moment awareness comes naturally to kids, and we adults usually do everything we can to screw it up for them. Kids know life should be fun. Kids know you should follow your bliss, engage in things that excite you, and learn whatever you are naturally inspired to learn in that moment.

My son will enthusiastically and quickly comprehend an impossibly worded manual for some advanced electronic device that I'd rather cut my foot off than attempt to operate. He's a skilled and avid videographer who seems to intuitively know how to use any complicated equipment related to this passion. But the basics of middle-school math elude him, the monumental burden of actually writing down and following through with homework assignments repeatedly proves insurmountable, and I still have to ask him to brush his teeth in the morning.

I confess that I've spent many years trying to "rehabilitate" Tuck—to cure him of his insistent present-moment tendencies so that he would more successfully fulfill teachers' and society's expectations of him. But he has proven himself incurable on that front. He is the funniest, kindest, most insightful, *happiest* person I've ever known, in spite of frequent academic failures and the ensuing consequences I impose on him. He simply, peacefully, refuses to expend any genuine effort or energy on anything that does not resonate with him. I still try—valiantly and in vain—to teach him the importance of caring about *all* of his schoolwork. But secretly, I'm envious . . . and a silent part of me cheers him on.

For most of us, living in the now requires lots of dedicated practice, and I'm far from an expert at it. Regular meditation helps more than anything. In daily life, whenever I catch myself ruminating or notice that I'm feeling distracted, I use that as a cue to re-center myself in the present moment. When my beautiful, loquacious preteen, Katy, asks a lengthy question and I blankly answer, "Huh?" I know it's time. Your thoughts are almost always about the past or the future, so the present moment is a *feeling* zone rather than a thinking zone.

I have a favorite way of accessing the now that I learned from spiritual master Eckhart Tolle. Treat yourself to a present-moment experience and try it with me *now:* Just decide, in this moment, to feel your divine self within your physical body. Focus on the sensation of life in your hands, your legs, your toes as you wiggle them. We take it for granted all the time, but it's a really cool sensation. Intentionally crank up your awareness of the buzzing vitality that animates every cell of your being.

I like to move and stretch, feeling the aliveness in my body and knowing that aliveness is my God-self. When you're focusing on the presence of your God-self inhabiting your form, you're automatically released from your mental activity. I like to acknowledge in that moment, too, that I extend beyond my body. I can feel the energy in my form, but the energy that is me actually extends beyond my physical self, and I can intentionally extend it as far as I please. As Tolle says, "Remind yourself to feel your inner body as often as you can. This alone, will help you to vibrate at ever higher vibrational frequencies and therefore you will attract new circumstances that reflect these higher frequencies."

If that's too freaky for you, just focus on your senses. What are you seeing, hearing, touching, right in this second? You can't focus on your senses while you're consumed with thoughts, so this automatically brings you into the present. Admire the juxtaposition of colors in your current surroundings. What does your underwear feel like against your skin right now? What does the person next to you smell like?

I'm a big fan of the tactile sense. As a mindfulness practice, I really enjoy touching my own skin or interesting fabrics or sticky things, and putting all my attention on the tactile sensations. My art-loving Katy's Play-Doh is perfect. So yielding, so compliant, so submissive, squishy and warm. Find some Play-Doh and just revel in the texture, the feel of it, that funky smell, those disturbing colors. Listen to it squish. Go ahead and taste it; I won't tell anyone. Take a vacation from your stories by dipping into the now as often as you can.

When you feel a story pulling at you, mentally take responsibility for having created that story by giving it your attention in the past. Make the deliberate decision to stop feeding it. Taking control of your conscious attention is the best tool you have for writing better stories going forward. Your attention is your *chi,* your life force, the dispenser for all your infinite potential for creation. Understanding that is the key to writing better stories.

Try this trick for managing the energy that could potentially create future victim stories.

NakedWriting for Nipping Victim Stories in the Bud

Whenever you recognize something new in your life that you don't like, do a NakedWriting on this prompt: *What must I be believing about myself or believing about the world to have created this circumstance?* Just shining light on the beliefs will go a long way toward dissipating their power.

Separate your *perception* of the event or circumstance from the facts that describe it, just like you did in the Just the Facts, Ma'am NakedWriting.

Brainstorm other possible perceptions you could deliberately choose to adopt in order to release your resistance toward this issue. Does it hold a valuable message for you? In some cases, your Judgment-Flipping skills will apply.

Find some thread of a reason to be thankful for this event or circumstance, and write the Universe a sincere note of gratitude.

Going Forward to Write Better Stories

Now that we've freed up some of your old, stuck energy, what kind of stories do you want to write from here on out? How can we make sure that we don't keep creating new victim stories?

Most of us have areas in our lives where we're *tolerating* things. And we get praised for that, right? We hear, "Suck it up! No pain, no gain! It could be worse!" But anytime we're tolerating something, it causes a slow, steady leak of our energy. It keeps us from being our brightest, best, most vital selves.

At first blush, tolerating may seem to resemble acceptance. It's actually the opposite. When we choose to accept and embrace a negative situation so that we can learn and grow from it, we allow the unwanted circumstance to move. We're giving ourselves fully to the emotion, and that's what keeps the *e* (energy) in *motion*. Tolerating is just a more subtle form of denying or repressing our emotions, and it keeps unwanted situations rigidly stuck in place.

For example, if you hate your job but all you do is complain about it, you're actually leaking heaps of your vital life force, your chi. And the funny thing is that you don't even have to quit that job to stop the energy leak. You just have to get real with yourself about it and take control of the situation. Simply making a clear decision that you will either leave that job or find a way to love it will seal up the leak, because in the moment you decide to stop *tolerating* a circumstance, you move into a position of power and positive forward movement. It doesn't matter how long it takes you to actually remedy the situation, as long as you've definitively decided that you will.

It's so easy to inadvertently fill our lives with conditions that are incompatible with our truest desires. It can be the people we're in relationships with, our occupations, our obligations to family or community. It's the most common cause of losing touch with your authentic inner voice. The more consistently you fail to listen to it, the dimmer the voice gets. People we call "emotionally un-available" are those individuals who have placed so much emphasis on the outer conditions of their lives that they've completely lost that connection with their deeper, truer identities. It becomes status quo for so many of us that it's almost considered normal in our society when it happens.

A Slow, Steady Leak

Juicy Joy student Lanie had a perfectly nice husband. But early on in their marriage, something changed—something that caused this marriage to fall short, in a significant way, of what Lanie had always imagined her marriage would be.

The specifics about what took place are not important. What's important is that throughout Lanie's life she had held a vision about what constituted a good marriage, and her marriage did not match her vision. She began tolerating aspects of her life with her husband. And since *tolerating* has a very specific effect on our energetic systems, it caused a slow, steady leak of her energy.

Now pretend that a marriage is a bicycle tire. Early in Lanie's marriage, the tire of her relationship sprung a leak. If this woman had been living as her true, authentic self, committed to her own Juicy Joy, she would have addressed this leak, immediately, and done whatever needed to be done to repair it.

But she wasn't living from that place. She was a people-pleaser. She didn't like to make waves. The bottom line was: she didn't feel she'd be loved if she made waves. She didn't feel deserving of love *unless* she put other people's needs above her own.

So the tire kept leaking air—her marriage kept leaking energy —year after year, as she *tolerated* this relationship that was good in many ways, but was truly not in keeping with her most cherished feelings about what it should be.

And I want to point something out here. There is no right or wrong when it comes to what people should expect to get out of a relationship. Lanie's husband thought that everything was great— *his* expectations were being met perfectly. You couldn't blame him for making it a bad marriage for Lanie; he was doing his part by being clear about his desires and making sure they were satisfied. But Lanie was not doing her part. She had not yet stepped into her glorious, gutsy self. So over time, this slow leak continued.

One day, Lanie realized the tire had gone totally flat. She panicked. And she started pumping air into the tire.

"Honey, we have to get into marriage counseling."

"I've signed us up for a couples' retreat."

"I've signed us up for *another* couples' retreat."

"I've signed us up for a sexuality retreat."

Lanie kept pumping, pumping, pumping air into the tire. Her husband was freaked out now, too, so he was pumping with her. It didn't seem to Lanie that he was ever pumping quite as frantically as she was, but he *was* pumping.

And as you'd imagine, with all that air going into the tire, it started to inflate. It never got nearly as firm as it was before the leak, but it made substantial improvement. And Lanie said, "Whew. Thank God, 'cause I'm exhausted."

It was a lot of work, all that pumping.

But guess what? As soon as Lanie stopped pumping like a maniac, it became painfully obvious that the leak was still there. The tire had been flat for so long that it had become irreparable, and all the air they had pumped into it leaked right back out. There's nothing that could save a bike tire at that point, and ultimately there was nothing that could save Lanie's marriage, so it ended. Relationships are energetic systems, and they need a constant flow of energy to survive. Without that flow, they die.

To keep a relationship strong—any kind of relationship—both people need to be ready to pump up the tire and seal off any leaks as soon as they're detected. Because even if a bike tire is halfway flat, or *almost* flat, you can usually pump it back up and be fine, right? But once it's completely flat and you've been riding around on it that way for a while, then your only options are to replace the tire . . . or to ride around for the rest of forever on an empty, spent rim. And some people do choose that second option, but it's not on the menu board for a Juicy-Joyful life.

It's time to look closely to see if you can identify any areas in which your outer circumstances do not match the energy of who you know yourself to be at your deepest core. Awareness of these areas is what will keep them from becoming your future victim stories. You might want to focus on relationships and career, since these are often the two areas we invest most of our energy in.

Don't feel guilty if you pull up some stuff you don't like about a relationship you're in. It won't mean that it's a doomed relationship. A relationship is only as strong as its weakest link. Finding the weak links and pulling them out into the light gives you the opportunity to mend them, thereby profoundly strengthening the relationship on the whole.

Conversely, you might become aware that the energetic nature of this relationship is not in keeping with who you truly are, and you might decide to reevaluate its place in your life. But don't be afraid of the examination. If the relationship you're in is right for you, examining it sooner rather than later will only make it better. We'll be looking more closely at relationships in the Gut-Dripping chapter.

NakedWriting: What Are You Tolerating?

In your journal, NakedWriting style, answer these questions: (1) Do your outer circumstances match the energy of who you know yourself to be at your deepest core? and (2) What are the aspects of your life that you're tolerating? (You may want to revisit the Juicy Joy pizza you drew in your journal at the start of your journey for inspiration.)

Did you come up with anything? Most of us have a few places where our circumstances don't match up with our truest selves. Our lives are works in progress, always. It wouldn't be any fun if we had the finished product already and we were done with all our evolving, right? But sometimes we have a lot. Sometimes doing this exercise leads us to wonder how we ever got to this point, so frightfully far from our original mark.

Don't judge yourself if that's the case. It's abysmally common in our culture to lose touch with what's real and important for us. The more you tolerate outer circumstances that are not compatible with your core self, the more you inevitably start to forget who that core self is, until you wake up one day in a life that's totally wrong for you.

If you discovered a lot of things that you're tolerating—or even if you just discovered one, but it's a biggie—you have to again ask yourself: *Why? What's my payoff?* The more clear and honest you can be, the more you'll be able to move this issue into the light of consciousness where you can own it and stop being run by it.

Perhaps there's a situation you've been complaining about, and you often find yourself thinking, *I wish it were different.* When you stop to examine why you haven't *made* it different and get clear about what the payoffs are, you might make the conscious choice to keep it the way it is for now. That doesn't mean that you won't ever commit to changing it. But when you *decide* that you're going to keep this in your life for the moment, it stops the energy leak. You've stopped resisting the situation, and you know that when you're ready to address it, you will. This small shift makes a huge difference in your capacity for authenticity and self-love.

Think of it in terms of resources. You have all this personal energy, prana, chi, that you can use in any way you choose. When you tolerate something, you're casting yourself as a victim and allowing that energy to just go to waste. It's valuable energy you could be putting toward your Juicy Joy. You have to reclaim it by stopping the leaks, so you can direct that energy into what will really make your heart sing.

When you get more practiced at paying attention to how energy feels in your body, you'll feel a discernable shift the moment you commit to plugging up a leak. It's like a sigh in your body, a relief. Even if there's some anxiety or uncertainty about what to do next, you can blend it with excitement and let it be there, because your energy body is telling you that you're on the right track.

This is very important: Once you make the decision to stop tolerating something, you must expect and allow the *better* something to come in. The fact that the tolerated situation was distressing to you is evidence enough that the Universe wanted you to put an end to it. Once you take that stand for yourself, you'll unleash Universal support that can appear so uncanny you might dismiss it as too good to be true.

It's not. The Universe was waiting for you to grow a pair so that it could swoop in with these precise coincidences and synchronicities to put you on Easy Street. In the next chapter, we'll be talking about the ways we subconsciously limit our own joy and abundance. For now, just accept this phenomenon as fact, and be on guard against it. Watch for tiny signs that the Universe is bringing you your dreams, and wildly celebrate every one. Trust them, believe in them, and give them each a happy dance.

Be an Outlaw

We all have, in our heads, a set of laws about the way things should be, and they were put there when we were kids by our parents, our religions, the social climates we grew up in. In his book *The Four Agreements,* don Miguel Ruiz calls our indoctrination into these laws the "domestication of the species." Carl Jung and the controversial Indian mystic Osho call it the development of "the persona."

But our soul-selves are not beholden to these sets of laws. And to some extent, our individual sets of laws can be pretty arbitrary, even if we don't at first see it that way. Left unexamined, these embedded rules can place restrictions on our Juicy Joy, and we need to dare to break our laws when our instincts guide us to.

When you were noting the things you tolerate, did you feel pressure to tolerate any of those circumstances because of some rule or social law you have attached to it? Mentally play around with breaking that law. What would happen if you did? Try to get in touch with whether or not it's a law that has true value for you at your core—at source level—or if it's just a habit, an assumption that's been programmed into your brain by your family or society.

What if you're tolerating a job you hate, for instance, and your dream is to find a career that makes you leap out of bed every morning jazzed, energized, and passionately committed to your profession? If there's a "law" in the arbitrary law book in your head that says you must earn X amount of dollars, or you must work within X miles of your current home, or you must work only certain hours . . . then you may just need to rewrite a few laws.

NakedWriting for Outlaws

Take out your journal now and look back at the NakedWriting you did on the things in your life you're tolerating. See if you can make a list of all of the laws or rules that might be associated with these issues. I'm not talking about the laws set forth by our nation —hopefully you're cool with those. Just whatever laws or rules make you feel you're supposed to tolerate this.

Look at the list of laws you've come up with, and see if you can separate the ones that deeply resonate with you from the ones that don't. Which ones were instilled in you by the cultural climate you grew up in? Out of those, are there any that are incompatible energetically with your deeper human knowing?

If you have some like that, dare to break them. Twist perceptions. Shatter absolutes. It's okay. You truly are the creator of the world you inhabit. Your laws are only there if you say so. Rewrite those laws, making them jibe with your core values.

The more you can trust yourself to rewrite your laws, the more free you'll feel, and the more passionate you'll be about pursuing your Juicy Joy. What if Martin Luther King, Jr., hadn't dared to break the social laws of his day? Or the suffragettes? History is filled with pioneers who proudly owned the fact that their human energies were not compatible with the social mores of the time.

Chances are, you won't need to make history. Just create your life and your world around the values that are most true for you, one tiny step at a time. I might keep my kids home from school on a Tuesday and give them ice cream for breakfast and take them to the beach if I feel like that's what we all need that day. The society I live in says they must go to school on school days. My core self doesn't agree.

I shared a cabin with two friends on a recent cruise. Due to a booking error, our three-person room had only two twin beds, so a cot was brought in. There was truly no place to put the folded-up cot during the day, and leaving it open left no room at all to navigate the cabin. My friends wanted to request a new room, but in a flash of inspiration I pulled the cot out onto the small balcony. Heaven!

Everyone on the cruise who heard about my chosen sleeping arrangement thought I'd lost my mind. But it was my very favorite part of the trip. Every night in my balcony bed (including the night I was rained upon) was a juicy-memorable experience. The night sky in the middle of the ocean is phenomenal. The waves, the moonlight, the shooting stars . . . it was exactly the kind of peaceful, solitary, soul-soothing downtime I craved after busy days of high-energy excitement and learning. I can't wait to cruise again and sleep under the stars, cramped quarters or not.

In the above example, I did check with the cabin steward to make sure I wasn't making anyone's life more difficult by my actions. Breaking my laws must be done with integrity and respect for others in order for it to align with my core self. But the more I listen to my inner promptings rather than conforming to expectations, the more fun I have.

Take Control of Your Story

Whether you consider yourself at a high point in your life right now or a low point, pull your perspective back far enough to recognize that throughout your life there have been high *and* low points. When you're reading a novel, that's a good thing, right? It wouldn't be that interesting if your character stayed at a comfortable, easy pace, without much drama. How long would you read before your boredom made you hurl the book against the wall?

Now imagine yourself as the main character in your own novel. If you're at a low point right now, what always comes next? What *has to* come next? You're headed for something better, right? Or maybe you haven't hit bottom yet and are headed for something worse before it gets better, but when that happens . . . when a character goes through a really rough patch, isn't the resulting high point especially awesome?

Literature does this because it's how life works. It's only fiction in the details; the literary structure follows that pattern because it's in our human wiring. (If you don't like books, think about the last ten movies you saw.) We respond to this story framework because it resonates deeply with our humanness. We know it's true.

If we choose to believe differently; if we create a belief system that goes, "Life sucks and then you die," then it's definitely possible to create that for ourselves. But most of us resonate with the ups-and-downs-of-life structure that we see mirrored in our literature and films.

So, back to *your* life. Your novel, your movie. I want you to see it in your mind's eye—or feel it, whichever works best for you. Note all the dips and peaks, and then use your imagination to project into your future. Your beliefs up to now are what created all the magnificent stuff you've had in your life, as well as the crap. We've been reprogramming your beliefs so that you can script the best possible coming chapters to the story of your life. Allow yourself to be loose and free and imagine beyond anything you've already thought about.

NakedWriting: Blurb Your Life

Once you have the continuation of your life story loosely mapped out in your head, open your Juicy Joy journal and write back matter for the novel. Writing in the third person will help you get the necessary distance.

Blurb your life: Include a brief sentence or reference for each major dip and peak, each obstacle you've overcome. Set the perspective on this as far into the future as you're comfortable with. Where do you want the novel to end? Could be on your deathbed, or maybe you want to leave the option open for a sequel. Novels don't always end at the end of the character's life, but they do tend to finish on a good note. They end with the character having evolved in a significant way that has led to some sort of permanently, vastly improved condition or some goal being reached. At a novel's conclusion, don't we usually feel good about where the character is headed? (Yes, I know it's possible to find novels where this isn't the case. Stop reading those.)

Story-Stripping in a Juicy Nutshell

People identify themselves through the stories they tell. Every story you've been carrying around was created by a belief and cemented through the repeated application of your conscious attention. Your attention is the energy that fed these stories. Your attention is the energy that will write every new story you live. At any moment, you can choose to reinvent yourself by paying deliberate attention to your stories and rewriting them in a way that raises your vibration to one of Juicy-Joyful anticipation for spectacular things to come.

In this step, you cleaned up the negative energy you'd been dragging around in your old victim stories, and you learned how to consciously create the best possible stories from here on out. You examined your life for energy leaks caused by situations you've been tolerating, and you rewrote some laws to better reflect your true core values.

You planned a new outline for the novel of your life. The work you've been doing so far on your Juicy Joy journey provides the catalyst for the kind of emotional growth spurt a character typically achieves in a novel, so writing a juicy-happy future for yourself is more than appropriate. This is your story now. Believe it, create it, and go live it.

Step Five will show you how . . .

STEP FIVE

TACO-FILLING

You've done so much juicy, fabulous work! You deserve to be rewarded, and this is the step you've been waiting for! Your outer landscape will always evolve in the direction set by your inner landscape. Now that you've gotten your inner world in tip-top shape, let's focus on bringing all that yummy deliciousness into your outer world.

It's a tragic fact of human nature that we all have a mysterious tendency to put a cap on how much joy and abundance we allow into our lives, never permitting ourselves "the whole enchilada." I prefer to use a taco for this analogy instead of an enchilada. And it has to be the crunchy kind, because I like the way the top stays open so that we can just keep filling it.

Taco-Filling is teaching ourselves to break through the set points we all have that determine just how good we can stand it, so we can stop subconsciously capping the amount of abundance we allow ourselves—whether it's abundance in love, respect, money, leisure time, or wherever we're feeling a lack.

Most of us have different set points for different areas of our lives, depending entirely upon what we believe, subconsciously, that we deserve. Some of us have a very high set point for money, but a low one for love. Or it could be the reverse. Or it could be lower than we'd like for both. We all know that it's not the amount of love, money, or what have you that we *want* that determines the amount we get. What we get is always determined by what we subconsciously believe we're worthy of. Your Juicy Joy journey thus far has been devised to shift those beliefs into self-loving overdrive, so if you've kept up diligently with your practices, you should be in great shape to fill your first taco.

My favorite part of the Taco-Filling Step is creating a Juicy Joy Reality Plan—an emotion-generated vision for your perfect life, whether you know exactly what that would look like already, or you're starting from a blank slate.

Filling our tacos with our Juicy Joy Reality Plans depends on first determining our truest desires on a core, soul level. Even though it's our human nature to keep returning to our set points, our conscious attention allows us to permanently recalibrate where they're set. What makes a great story, novel, or movie so inspiring and satisfying is that usually, at the end, the character has effectively upgraded his or her set point, right?

Good thing you've had so much practice with all your Juicy-Feels, because we're going to do some powerful pretending in this step to solidly anchor your Juicy Joy Reality Plan and position it as the new filter through which you'll perceive the world.

Instincts and You

Imagine a bird in a cage in the springtime. All of the bird's biological needs are comfortably met. He is well cared for by owners who love him, keep his cage clean, and practice all of the very best pet-care policies. But the bird feels a stirring in him that he doesn't understand. It seems that he should be *doing* something. He doesn't know what it is because he's never built a nest, found a mate, migrated, or searched for worms in his whole life, yet there's some longing in him to work and create and follow his instincts—a longing he's unable to satisfy or even explore.

The bird's anguish is your anguish and my anguish. All of the interwoven layers of our crappy filters have built our cages. We couldn't connect with our natural human instincts and intuition because they were buried, along with our true core selves, beneath those layers. But with awareness and conscious effort, we've begun to peel back the layers. We can now strain to hear our faint, stifled inner voices. Unlike the imprisoned bird, we can choose to open the cage and liberate ourselves to fulfill our instinctual destinies.

The exercises you've been doing along your Juicy Joy journey have cleared a path to your deeply buried instinctual nature. You may be faintly aware of a new energy building up inside you. It's time to focus on that new energy and intentionally amplify it so you can ride it into your well-deserved Juicy Joyful future.

Think of the iconic stereotypes that captivate the attention and imagination of young people. Outlaws. Pirates. Vampires. What makes these caricatures so attractive is their raw lustiness for life and their powerful determination to satisfy their base instincts—such a stark contrast to the restriction-laden existence we all contend with as payment for inclusion in our society.

It's no wonder children and teens are generally more enchanted by these types of stories than adults are. They haven't had as long to become anesthetized to their deepest instincts to live fully and freely, sucking the marrow from life and blissfully operating from their authentic core beings. They haven't had as much time to absorb the mass-mentality fear of raw, uncensored expression that permeates our cultural climate.

Your pursuit of Juicy Joy hereby gives you license to unearth your outlaw nature. To release that scurrilous, denied piece of you; to exalt it, love it, and then—only then—to blend and balance it with the other bits of you that comprise a full, vital human being.

Have you ever burst into tears at the beauty of a sunset? Would you like to?

Many years ago when my kids were young, I had an epiphany about the origin of the caps we put on our happiness. We had been waiting for almost a year for our turn to stay at the brand new Animal Kingdom Lodge that had just opened at Disney World. My son, who was seven at the time, was just a tremendous animal lover. He had jungle scenes painted all over his room, stuffed-animal monkey collections, the works. My daughter, Katy, then three years old, had naturally caught the contagious excitement, and she knew that something really spectacular was waiting for us on this vacation.

We checked in kind of late and went out on our balcony, and I think we saw a deer off in the distance, but nothing really amazing that first night. The hotel was set up in a U-shape, with a Disney-esque African savannah in the middle where the animals would make appearances. Trees were beyond the savannah, for the times when they didn't feel like socializing. We'd been told that the best time to see the animals was morning, so we went to sleep.

Being three, my daughter was the first one awake the next morning. I picked her up, and since I didn't want her to wake up my son, I decided to take her out on the balcony for a while. I pulled back the curtain, and saw the most spectacular display of animals. There was a watering hole where they'd come to drink— giraffes, zebras, all kinds of antlered creatures.

I stepped out onto the balcony with Katy, and she slowly lifted her sleepy head. It took her a moment to process everything. Then she just lit up with crazy excitement and shouted "AMINALS!"— causing every single animal to jump in sudden terror and bolt off into the trees.

They were gone.

I heard this broad, collective moan, and for the first time I noticed that everyone who was staying at the Animal Kingdom Lodge had come out onto their balconies to witness this silent, reverent, morning gathering of the whole menagerie.

I said, "Katy, honey, you scared them away . . ."

Her sweet face just crumbled. Huge tears spilled out of her eyes.

And then I teared up, too, as I realized that it was my embarrassment about all the people on their balconies that caused me to say that to her. All she was doing was expressing her joy and excitement over something that was so wonderful to her. I should have been helping her feel better about what happened, not worse.

And I thought about how I do that to my kids, all the time—how we all do it, even in our mundane, day-to-day activities. When my son was young, for instance, he would express his joy at the beach by running, full-out, as fast as he could down the shoreline. And what would I do? I'd stop him and call him back.

Similarly, my daughter used to express the joy she got from her spaghetti by standing up in her chair in the restaurant to sing and dance about it. And of course, I'd make her get down. Just think about how many times in an average day we ask children to *rein in* the natural joy and enthusiasm they're feeling!

It is inevitable, under these conditions, that a child would form the subconscious belief that "feeling and expressing my joy full-out is wrong, wrong, wrong." It is inevitable that a child would start to subconsciously equate his unbridled enthusiasm with feelings of unease so that whenever a situation felt too good, too joyous, he would subconsciously feel a need to cap that happiness before it made anyone upset.

My point is not about whether or not parents should do this, but about acknowledging that this *is* one of the ways we routinely indoctrinate our offspring into our culture. This is how every one of us grew up, whether we had fantastic parents or awful ones. For some of us, the message was more barbed than it was for others, but the way our society is structured, it's unlikely that any of us escaped this message or escaped forming the filter-muddying beliefs it generates.

What's Your Set Point?

Imagine that it's a steamy-hot summer day and you're sitting in your bedroom with the air-conditioning on, perfectly comfortable. You have the thermostat set exactly where you want it. Then someone opens the window, and hot air starts pouring in. Your bedroom can get pretty balmy pretty quick. But then what would your air conditioner do? Your thermostat is set to maintain a specific temperature, so your air conditioner is going to automatically crank itself up to try to compensate. The longer the window stays open, the harder the air conditioner is going to work to bring the temperature back to the set point.

Same with our metabolic set points, right? We might go on a really strict diet and get to be fashionably twiggy for a while, but eventually our metabolism makes sure we go right back to our natural set-point weight. Or we go on a cruise and gain six pounds, but after a while our metabolism pulls our weight back down. We have money set points as well. We've all heard about the billionaires who lose everything in some big gamble, then within a year they're billionaires again. And we've heard about the lottery winners who ended up right back where they started a few years later.

We have a set point for joy, too. We might have good weeks or months, or bad weeks or months, but usually we level off from our highs and lows at roughly the same place. *Until now.* We're going to raise the set point on our thermostats for Juicy Joy! To do that, we're going to need to know two things clearly. We'll need to know where our thermostat is currently set, and we'll need to decide where we *want* to set it. We're going to be charting a course, and just like when you do so on a GPS system, you can't get anywhere until you plug in an accurate start point and a precise end point.

Take an objective inventory of the circumstances that comprise your life. That's the truest indicator of where your thermostat has been set. Maybe you're really happy with certain things, and you don't have to mess with the thermostat on those. But if there are areas of your life where you're simply not getting the results you want, those are the areas where the set point on your joy thermostat needs to be bumped up. Usually, we can look back and see that our results in any specific category have been pretty constant, overall, throughout our lives. We may have had some high moments and low moments, but for the most part, it's been pretty steady.

Now that you have an idea of where your set points are, we're going to permanently raise them by identifying and cleaning up any lingering limiting beliefs that could potentially keep them stuck.

NakedWriting: But-List

Take out your Juicy Joy journal, and think of the one thing you most want that you don't have. Write the words: "I want _____, *but . . .*" (filling in the blank with the thing you want).

Then, NakedWriting style, write down everything that comes to mind for you, after the "but." It might sound like this: "I want to start my own business, *but* it takes a ton of capital to start a business, and it would be nuts in this economy to try to launch something, and I don't have the right education or job training for the kind of business I want to start. Plus, I'm too old . . . blah, blah, blah."

Everything you wrote down after the "but" is a sneaky, limiting belief you're still carrying around. It doesn't matter how "true" they are. We know that there is no objective reality. Reality is simply what we perceive and what we create based on those perceptions. Anytime you hear yourself shirking away from your dream with a "but," remember this wise counsel: "Limiting beliefs come out of your but(t)."

Your but-reasons are showing you where your thermostat is currently set on achieving that particular thing you want. The next thing to begin thinking about is: Where would you *like* it to be set? What level of Juicy Joy do you want to experience? It doesn't need to be a detailed picture of the circumstances. If you have some clear circumstance in mind, that's fine, but try to identify what the *feeling* is that you believe that circumstance will bring you, and understand that the feeling itself is what you really desire.

If you do want to put some circumstance into this new set point, make sure it's one that really makes your heart sing. Don't pick a practical goal. Let's say, for instance, that you want to improve your finances. You've been a real-estate agent for 20 years, so the most practical thing that would improve your finances would be a few really big sales. If the thought of that excites you *beyond* the relief of the financial gain, great. Use that.

But if you're choosing it simply because it seems like the most likely way for you to increase your income, open up the possibilities. Maybe you're over real estate, but you've been thinking lately that it would be so cool to sell boats . . . or learn acupuncture! Or maybe there's one aspect of real estate that you've put your own personal stamp on that does excite you. Maybe you'd be excited about *teaching* other Realtors this particular strategy, and that's where you could put your career focus. Really feel into the possibilities, and look for cues from your body that you've hit on a joy nerve. Don't make this about your past. Make it about your future, with all its unlimited potential. If any ideas are coming to you already, jot them down in your journal.

When you're deciding where to set your joy thermostat, it's good to brainstorm role models. Models can help you to clarify what you want and prove to your more skeptical side that it's possible to have what you're dreaming of. If someone else is having it, it must be possible, right? Take a moment to see if you can think of anyone you know personally, or you've observed in the media or whatever, who has what you want in that area of life. If you can't come up with anyone, invent such a person in your imagination.

NakedWriting: Who's Got It?

Holding this person in your thoughts, make a list in your journal of the kinds of beliefs that you would imagine make up that person's filter.

If you're picturing someone you know well, you might have a pretty good idea what the belief systems are like. But if you aren't clear on what the underlying beliefs would be, make a list of all the habits this person has—or probably has—just from what you know about him or her. What does he do on a daily basis? How does she interact with others? Where does she go? What does he buy? What does he wear? What does she eat? How does he walk?

Once you've written down everything you can think of about this person, use that list to speculate what underlying beliefs might be at work. For purposes of this exercise, accuracy isn't all that important; it's okay to just guess.

Now, look at your but-list. Project your buts onto this person. If this person had your limiting beliefs, could she have ever accomplished such a high level of success in this one area of life? This exercise is not meant to encourage you to abandon your authenticity in order to copy the habits of another. It's meant to shine a light on those very last beliefs that may be holding you back from adopting habits you would authentically enjoy and benefit from! Just bringing the crappy beliefs into your awareness takes a huge bite out of their power.

So let's get the limiting beliefs out of there. They're energy, right? They're not anything more substantial than that. And we have the power, with our minds, to change the vibration of the energy we inhabit or that inhabits us. In the past, we've accepted the vibration of our mucky filters because we didn't realize we had that power. But we now understand that we are sovereign masters over our energy and can take control of it just by acknowledging that.

NakedWriting: Why It's Mine

In your Juicy Joy journal, list all the reasons you absolutely *will* be able to attain the thing you most desire. They might sound like this:

- *I've had it before, or something close to it.*
- *I have xyz-skills that could help me attain this.*
- *I have a supportive spouse/friend/lover.*

- *I have experienced the contrast that now allows me to clearly know what I want.*

- *I've overcome obstacles greater than this before.*

- *When I fully align myself with my passion, the Universe will step in with divine assistance I can't even yet imagine.*

- *I am smart and capable.*

- *I've never fully committed to attaining a goal before, so I actually have no idea how resourceful and resilient I can be.*

When you think you're done, push yourself to write ten more reasons. Remember that you are Mirror You, and write your list from that perspective. Don't get caught up this time in trying to reverse all the items on the but-list. Some of them may be irreversible. That doesn't mean they have to keep you from your goals. Then put your models on this list. ("He has it, so it's possible to have this," and so on.)

Read this list out loud, with juicy excitement, every night just before you go to sleep and every morning as soon as you wake up. Even if you have to fake the juicy excitement sometimes.

Love Your Fear

Look at your but-list one last time. What emotion underlies all of your buts? In almost every case, the bottom-line emotion that keeps us from our dreams is fear. Fear shows up in myriad disguises to hold us back from our juicy life. Most people do not go full-out for the things they want, and the biggest reason they don't is a fear of failing—a fear that they'll go full-out and it won't be enough. So they don't even try. And that's why there are so few people actually living their dreams. The ones who *are* living their dreams are the ones who have learned to successfully Emotion-Mix their fear with excitement and joy.

Just like all our other emotions, fear is only energy. Over and over in this book, we've seen that the only way to work with an undesirable energy is to accept it. Rather than trying to vanquish it, we who know the secrets of Juicy Joy embrace our fear, and that's how we get it on our side. When we resist anything, what happens? Come on, say it with me: *What we resist persists.*

Fear is almost always going to come up when you're trying for something new in your life. We have this cultural thing in our filters that says fear is a sign we should retreat. But we can rewire that so fear is a sign that we should get excited and rally our internal resources to move forward, through the fear, to the really awesome thing that's just beyond it.

Fear and excitement have very similar biological responses. There are a tiny few instances in our lives when fear actually *is* a signal to retreat, and dropping into our intuition with an honest inquiry will tell us when that's the case. But the vast majority of the things we fear are the results of the limiting beliefs we've accumulated. We fear embarrassment, abandonment, vulnerability, loss of security. In all of these cases, if we're able to be with our fear, welcome it, be curious about it, pull back and look at it from what Buddhists call the "witness perspective," we can usually use our Emotion-Mixing skills to blend enough excitement into it to make it feel good.

When you allow yourself to be afraid and excited at the same time, it's kind of juicy. Dramatic people naturally get this concept. Not the drama-queen types who get off on their misery, but the dramatic people who just seem to know that life is a breathtaking adventure and wouldn't have it any other way. Fear is nothing more than an expectation of something bad happening. It's just your imagination, so you can take control of it. If you have faith that everything that happens to you is supposed to happen—even the "bad" things—then fear becomes obsolete.

When you feel afraid, try blending the fear with these thoughts and the feelings they produce: *I welcome this fear because it's here for my benefit. Whatever happens, that will be for my benefit, too. I will learn from this, I will grow from this, and if I remain aware and welcoming of its message, it will ultimately be a stepping-stone to greater joy for me. Yay, fear!* Most of what we fear never happens anyway. And the more we resist the things we fear, the more likely we'll be to attract them.

Being with your fear allows it to move. When you resist or restrict it, it gets stuck, and that's how you get immobile in your life. An instructor at a transformative self-dev program where I regularly assist (The Living Course) tells a story about being in a hot tub at a resort one evening and observing the following interaction between a young boy and his father.

It was dark and the hot tub was making lots of noise, and as they approached it the little boy told his dad he was scared. Without missing a beat, the dad said, "Okay. Let's say hello to the fear." The little boy waved apprehensively and said, "Hello, fear!" Then the dad unceremoniously led the boy into the hot tub. They swam around for a while and when he was ready, the boy, unprompted, said, "Good-bye, fear!" and proceeded to have a great time.

This conscious dad didn't try to reason his son's fear away or make it wrong. Together they acknowledged it, greeted it warmly, and never even considered the possibility that fear might be a reason to change their plans. With this kind of training, I can't imagine the boy having anything less than an adventure-filled, Juicy-Joyful life.

Hating our fear, denying our fear, or letting our fears run us all have the unwanted effect of freezing the fear in our energy systems. It becomes concentrated, gains strength, and gets increasingly difficult to move. But when you give fear room—when you let it breathe—it naturally thins out and becomes ever easier to blend with more enjoyable emotions like anticipation, exhilaration, and pride.

It's a good idea to train yourself to enjoy fear because it's going to precede just about every big step you take toward your Juicy Joy. And it's almost never a reason to stay out of the hot tub.

Passion Trumps Fear

When it comes to chasing down a dream, the trick is not to vanquish fear, but to override it with passion. When you want something bad enough, fear simply becomes a nonissue. On a vision board I once made, I'd clipped a magazine headline that said: I'M AFRAID TO MAKE CHANGES. BUT I'M MORE AFRAID NOT TO. If you feel fear about moving toward your dream, take stock of how much you're giving up by not taking that step. Love yourself enough to start fearing *that* more.

When I asked the acclaimed intuitive teacher Denise Linn for a tip about living authentically, she said, "It's better to do something in an imperfect way than to do nothing faultlessly. If you never plant the seed, it can't grow and blossom." Authentic living equals authentic *doing*. What actions would you be taking toward your dreams if fear of failure did not exist in your consciousness?

We're going to do just a few more NakedWriting exercises to get some clarity before we create the Juicy Joy Reality Plans we'll stuff our tacos with.

NakedWriting: If Only . . .

In your journal, make a list of everything you wish had been given to you or done for you in your childhood. Don't overthink it; just jot down the first things that come to mind. Your list may have tangible items on it, or it may have intangibles like "encouragement to follow my dreams" or "compassion for my limitations."

Make your list now.

If specific, tangible items are on your list, ask yourself, "Why did I want this?" and see if you can translate each item to the feeling you were after. For instance, if you have some trendy clothing item on your list, the feeling might have been "to fit in with the crowd," "to be accepted," or "to feel important."

These are your unmet needs. Even though we are often completely unaware of them, we are all driven by our unmet needs. They aren't bad, and we don't necessarily have to get rid of them.

To a large extent, they determine who we are. Becoming conscious of our unmet needs and finding ways to satisfy them for ourselves can become a juicy component of our paths. See if you can identify a common thread that connects your unmet needs. For example, when I do this exercise, it's apparent that what I missed out on most as a child was feeling truly *seen*. My primary unmet needs were:

1. Feeling that my thoughts and opinions mattered.

2. Feeling free to speak my truth without fear of rejection or ridicule.

3. Feeling deeply, authentically connected with others.

Becoming aware of my unmet needs helped me understand why I'd been drawn in certain directions in my life, and to be more forgiving and loving of myself. I recognize that those are the unmet needs that make me want to write books like this one, to speak, and to lead retreats and online training programs that have a profound impact on people's lives. I've found a way to shape my natural drive to have these needs met into a career I absolutely love. Maybe at some point these needs will be satiated and I'll be drawn to a completely different career or passion. Unmet needs can be a blessing when we figure out how to direct them into something positive. Often they're the underlying fuel for our passions.

Funny story: My son, Tuck, who was 12 at the time, was at one of my Juicy Joy workshops when we did this exercise. He got busy right away with his NakedWriting on "What do you wish had been given to you or done for you in your childhood?" Within moments, he silently held his notebook up for me to see. In big block letters that took up the whole page, he'd written: I-PAD. This exercise was not designed for 12-year-olds.

Do You Have Passion for Your Passion?

What is your *passion?* If you don't have a ready answer, that's okay. Most people don't. But the ones who do have a ready answer to that question are typically living more Juicy-Joyful lives. When you have a clear bead on what you want, combined with confident expectation and unswerving dedication to getting it, the whole journey becomes meaningful and enjoyable.

According to Steve Martin's memoir, *Born Standing Up,* he spent 14 years learning and perfecting the art of stand-up comedy before he began achieving any measurable success at it whatsoever. He had no way of knowing, during any of those long years of hard work, the kind of fame that would eventually come to him. He just knew he had to follow his passion, and he was driven to stay focused on that dream. He had "natural diligence," which he describes as the ability to not become distracted by anything that was not related to his goal. He made his whole life about pursuing his passion, and there was no way he wouldn't eventually succeed.

I got this joke from the author Sherman Alexie: Why did Native American rain dances always work? Because the Native Americans kept dancing until it rained. *Da-dum.* When you get clear about what your passion is, you're able to streamline and simplify, and not get bogged down by juggling a bunch of unrelated, and therefore unnecessary, commitments. You can enjoy the *working toward* the goal almost as much as achieving it, because the whole effort feels so *right* to you.

If you don't know what your passion is, you could even decide to become passionate about discovering your passion! Here's what you *don't* do: You don't think about your life and try to pick something to assign as your passion. If your passion were already in your life, you'd know it. And you don't go crazy frantically searching for your passion either. Instead of trying to find your passion, you have to let your passion find you.

But you do have to *help* it find you, and one of the most powerful ways to do so is to carve out some free time for yourself. There's a principle in feng shui that says you have to make space to allow anything new into your life. You can't pour water into a full cup; for something new to enter, you have to make room for it. That principle applies here. To open up space for your passion-finding mission, do an honest appraisal of the ways in which you spend your time, and be brutal about cutting out the time sucks that are the least in keeping with who you are. Remember the list you made of the parts of your life you're tolerating? Figure out which ones you'd be most willing to eliminate, and use the time from those to leisurely explore your new potential passions. This can be a difficult step, but it's so important for your self-love!

Then invite the Universe to lead you to your passion and simply go about your day with the expectation that something different will catch your eye. Watch for an ad for a concert, seminar, or group you wouldn't normally pay attention to. Listen to a commercial on the radio for a product you wouldn't normally buy. Once you make a conscious decision to open to new opportunities, you'll be amazed to realize how much you ordinarily close yourself off to, just out of habit. Make a commitment to expose yourself to everything that holds the slightest bit of curiosity for you. Follow every thread to see where it leads. The hardest part of this practice for most people is the initial step of making the time for it.

You can't decide on a passion because it's convenient, or your new girlfriend shares it, or it fits in your budget. Your only reliable guide is your gut. A true passion is often *not* sensible. It will fill you up with thoughts, feelings, or ideas about it. It will give you a rush of energy. And you'll feel a *rightness* when you're involved with it that can be hard to explain to others. According to Pema Chödrön, "Everything in our lives can wake us up or put us to sleep, and basically it's up to us to let it wake us up." I would add that it's also up to us to *find* the things that wake us up.

You could have a passion for your career, a cause you believe in, a group you belong to, or simply a hobby. You don't *have* to have a passion right now to have a Juicy-Joyful life or a crunchy taco that's filled to the brim with good stuff. But take a few moments to center yourself and feel into your gut. Ask the wiser part of you, "If

I had to guess what my passion might be, I'd say _____."
Write any thoughts in your journal.

Taco-Loading 101

Just like in the Mirror You JuicyFeel when you got to meet your ideal self, you're about to meet your ideal life. Without any concern for what seems practical or realistic, how would you like your life to look? As you continue reading, just start to consider what the "whole enchilada" might be for you.

Try not to fall back on the things that you imagine anybody would pick, like millions of dollars. If you think you want millions of dollars, ask yourself: *Why? What would that mean for me, specifically —for the life I want to create?* Unlike a lumpy, sealed-up, finite enchilada, your taco is open and limitless. You can put a whole list of things in there, or just a few cherished dreams. You'll be adding to it for the rest of your life, so don't feel pressured to figure it all out right now.

You decide what goes into your taco. Period. No one else gets a say; this is *your* taco to fill. I want you to be very self-centered about this and very much aware of the power you have to choose anything you'd like. We talked in the last chapter about that subconscious list of laws we all have in our heads. Now is the time to break every one of the laws you've been obeying that does not jibe with your core essence.

If your taco is full of easy, nonrisky, pleasant stuff, you're not understanding what this crunchy treat represents. Tacos are spicy! They're scarily messy to eat. You'll probably get a blotchy salsa stain on your shirt—but you won't give a crap about your stupid shirt because this taco is *so good.*

My Taco

I'm going to give you an example of something I once put in my taco that no one thought I'd ever be able to get. Even when I was perfectly clear and ecstatic in my plan, every person I told about it rolled their eyes and thought I was nuts. If I hadn't cranked up my own inner voice loud enough to drown out the voices around me, I never would have been able to create this beautiful filling for my taco, which has now exceeded my expectations in every way.

This particular taco-stuffing took place as my marriage was winding down, so here's the background on that: Greg is a warm, kind, smart, generous, and all-around wonderful man, but our marriage had stopped working for me. We'd both been playing out exactly what we were drawn together to play out for the symbiotic furthering of our souls' paths. I'd been attracting from him the exact treatment I'd been historically comfortable receiving based on a lifetime of insecurity and people-pleasing. Greg had been thoughtlessly acting out the fears and unconscious attitudes that permeated his filter as a result of his own lifetime of accumulated experiences. With this combination of factors in place, my continuous journey into ever-greater authenticity and self-love had inevitably led me to fall out of love with him.

With the help of several years of marriage counseling and many personal-development and relationship courses, we were able to overcome old patterns and significantly strengthen our partnership with the exception of one vital component: I could never reawaken the romantic attraction I had once felt for Greg. I adored him as an important person in my life, but I could not access the deep-connection feelings of marriage-style love with him. It was a tremendous test of my authenticity and self-acceptance to finally admit this. I tried everything possible to turn it around, but the one thing I would not allow myself to do was to become inauthentic about it.

Once I knew without a doubt that I would never again feel romantically inclined toward this man, the only authentic course of action seemed to be divorce. But for a long time, divorce just did not feel right. Ironically, all of that counseling and personal-development work we'd done together had brought us to an impasse. We'd reached such a level of compassion and understanding toward one another and become such close friends that it seemed crazy to make such a dramatic change to our lives. Even though the romantic and sexual aspects of our union were indisputably over, we both cherished day-to-day family life with our two fantastic tweenage children.

I had bought into society's picture about how divorce is supposed to look, and I couldn't bear the thought of dragging our children back and forth between our separate homes. I couldn't bear the thought of dividing up all the things we were so happily sharing, or ending relationships with one another's families. I couldn't even bear the thought of not seeing Greg on a regular basis. I truly loved combining forces with him on parenting and household responsibilities, laughing with him, and socializing together with our mutual friends. I didn't want to give those things up, but I didn't want to give up the possibility of ever again having a deeply connected romantic partnership in my life either. It was a heartbreaking decision—one I spent hundreds of middle-of-the-night hours crying over.

I was teaching Juicy Joy, and I knew that staying in a friendship-only marriage was not something I could authentically embrace. I am a passionate person. I love Love. I love big, lusty, voracious, capital-L Love. It seemed bitterly unfair to me that I should have to sacrifice something so intrinsic to my character in order to keep my family together.

I finally realized during one of those middle-of-the-night sob-fests that I was subscribing to a law about the definition of divorce that did not jibe with what I felt, authentically, in my core being, made sense. It was a law put there by the society I belonged to, not one that resonated with my inner truth. Relief and excitement! I vowed, in that moment, that I would have it all.

I got enthusiastically creative in filling my taco. I broke rules. I decided that I would *not* dissolve our family simply because I needed to dissolve our marriage. I got very specific about rewriting the rules of divorce to suit my particular situation. Who said my divorce had to look like my friends' divorces, or had to even remotely resemble any other divorce ever in the entire history of divorces?

Obviously, this dream required two people to share the vision, and Greg was initially reluctant to get on board with my creativity, because he did not want the divorce at all. He was horrified by my decision. My self-love and dedication to my authenticity was put to the ultimate test. Oriah whispered to me at night: "I want to know if you can disappoint another to be true to yourself."

Yes, Oriah. Yes. It's so unfathomably unnatural to me that it hurts like hell, but I believe I finally can.

I filled my taco with my Juicy Joy Reality Plan, which included keeping the kids' lives as unchanged as possible by having them remain full-time residents of the house we all love—with Greg and me alternating time there with them—and all of us continuing to spend ample fun time together as a foursome. I rewrote the definition of "family," so that parents who were no longer married to one another could remain a family unit with their children. I did all of the processes, JuicyFeels, and exercises you're about to learn to solidify my vision and make my taco a reality.

My resolve opened the floodgates to divine assistance. Miracles occurred daily. And I did get to have it all. Our divorce was sad, of course, and we all allowed ourselves the full expression of our sadness about it. But ultimately it was a dream divorce—nothing more than a peaceful, gentle relabeling of our continuing friendship, which remains supportive and joyful and full of family-style love.

What I feared would be a terrible ordeal for my children, Greg, and me turned out to be the best possible thing for all of us. Those years I spent trying to fit myself into a mold that was no longer authentic for me were years that I was unable to be my best self and offer my best to others. Only after reclaiming and honoring my authentic self was I able to once again be the exceptional mom, daughter, sister, friend, and teacher that I knew I could be.

Until we've given ourselves what we most authentically need, we have nothing of value to give to anyone else.

Creating a Juicy Joy Reality Plan for Your Taco

Ready to create a template for your perfect life? Maybe you know just what that would look like already, and maybe you have no idea. Either way, we're going to get you some clarity now. What would you do if you knew you could do anything?

Get up and stretch for a moment. Wiggle those hips. Feel your energy pulsing in your body, and move in whatever way feels best to you. Then get super comfortable in your seat, and allow yourself to absorb these wise words by author Mike Dooley, which appear in his book *Notes from the Universe:*

> The reason you're "here" is not to be good, to be better, to be perfect, to get "stuff" done, to save the world, to save somebody, to prove something, or to be anything . . . other than yourself. That's all you have to work on. That's all you can do. But by doing it . . . all those other things will happen anyway. Your wishes are what the Universe wishes for you. Your thoughts steer the ship of your dreams. And no matter where you've "been," or how challenging your circumstances, right here and now is all that matters.

These next bits of NakedWriting are critical to your Juicy Joy journey, so make sure to be as naked, raw, and uncensored as you can possibly be.

NakedWriting: Your Taco Load

In your journal, answer this question: *If I could magically freeze my regular life for one week without any consequences, and had every resource in the world available to me, what would I do with my time?* (You can handpick whichever aspects of your regular life you'd like to incorporate into this fantasy.) Don't be practical! Be frivolous and indulgent. What would bliss you out? Do that now.

I want you to really dig deep for this next one. Bringing any insights you gleaned from the last question, you're going to write the words, *What I really want is . . . ,* and allow anything that comes up to flow effortlessly onto the paper. It might resemble your responses to earlier exercises, but allow for the possibility that your desires may have shifted or grown. Don't get up in your head! Feel the responses bubble up from within your body and just keep writing *What I really want is . . .* again and again, without letting your pen leave the paper, until you feel completely satisfied that there's nothing left. Whatever comes up is perfect, so don't try to get it right. Just listen to your inner voice and record what it says. Write for at least 20 minutes. Longer is fine.

Are you surprised by what came out? What we think we want isn't always what we want on a core, soul level. Are your desires mostly tangible or intangible? If you constructed vivid, detailed scenarios, or came up with lots of tangible items you want, spend some time now to disassemble them just a bit. Get underneath the specifics and tap into the *feelings* you believe you would have if these desires were to come to fruition. For each item, ask yourself: *Why do I want this?* If that still doesn't bring you to a core feeling, ask, *Why would that be good?* or *What would that get me?* Eventually these questions will lead you to the thing you most authentically want, like *I'd feel loved,* or *I'd feel valuable,* or *I'd feel safe,* or *I'd know I was making a difference in the world.* Write the core *feelings* in your journal.

Next, you're going to close your eyes and spend a few minutes pretending, powerfully, that you are already living this perfect life of your choosing. Reach back in your consciousness to the way you used to pretend when you were a kid, when you could try on any identity that struck your fancy and become it for the pretend game you were playing. Really anchor the feeling in. Feel the chemical change in your body.

You're going to consolidate all of this into a Juice Statement now, based on your true, deep wants. Look at everything you wrote, and see if you can boil it all down to its essence. What's underneath the trappings of what you believe you want? What lies at the guts of what you're after?

Now write down two or three or four words that capture this feeling. Phrase those words into a statement that begins with *I am.* . . . Take your time with this and make sure that every word you've chosen strikes a profound chord within you. You'll feel the rightness of it when you hit upon the perfect words. My statement is: *I am powerful, passionate, and free.*

Loudly proclaim your Juice Statement. (Or if you're at Starbucks, proclaim it loudly inside your head.) Do you feel a sense of expansion in your body? When you've captured the essence of what really excites you, you'll feel electricity in it. It's not just words. This statement will now represent the totality of your current Juicy Joy Reality Plan—everything you want for yourself. You've just filled your first taco.

Starting now, this phrase—this Juice Statement—is your *primo seed.* Water the hell out of it! You've got to latch onto this thing like you've never latched onto anything before. These words should guide your life. This isn't just about following your bliss, but energetically *claiming* your bliss, right here, right now—feeling unshakably confident in your ability to choose it and therefore have it. It's knowing, irrefutably, that you are truly holding the reins on your life and steering it where you want it to go. From now on you will behave as though your Juicy Joy Reality Plan were your current day-to-day reality. And soon it will be.

Close your eyes and vividly imagine your Juice Statement printed repeatedly on an endless streamer of Divine Love, and wrap that streamer around your energetic being again and again. This declaration is now irrevocably imprinted on the filter that determines your perception of the world, therefore your filter must attract results to match it.

It makes every decision ridiculously simple. *Should I buy that? Go there? Date her? Eat that? Well, let's see . . . does it align with my Juicy Joy Reality Plan?* Yes or no—there's your answer. Use your body! That feeling of expansion you get from your Juice Statement means the answer is yes. If you're unsure, or you feel more of a sense of contraction in your body, it's a no.

Another Self-Love Note

Are you still reading your love notes to yourself every time you see them on your mirror? Good! Add to them now. Write your Juice Statement under your affirmations and declare it with juicy, juicy feeling as often as you can.

JuicyFeel: Mirror You Living Your Juicy Joy Reality Plan

— Take all the steps to leisurely enjoy your Mirror You JuicyFeel.

— As your perfect self, after Mirror You has stepped into your being, notice a passageway or gate or doorway in your nature setting. Whatever comes up for you is perfect.

— Walk toward the passageway with giddy anticipation, knowing your ideal life is on the other side.

— Step into the world of your Juicy Joy Reality Plan. As Mirror You, your perfect self, revel in the full enjoyment of every aspect of this world.

— If the desires of your Juicy Joy Reality Plan are difficult to combine, you can spot an additional doorway or more, each representing another aspect of your Reality Plan, but be sure to spend plenty of time with each one.

— Make this the best possible experience or experiences you can imagine for yourself. It should feel so good that you never want to leave.

Can you feel it in your body? The excitement? The joy? The gratitude for this incredible life you're living? It's critical that you feel it as though you're already experiencing it. I'm sorry to have to break it to you, but if you can't get that kind of bliss going right now, in your own imagination, *you don't stand a chance of getting it in your real life.*

Go to the imaginary world of your Juicy Joy Reality Plan every night as you fall asleep. Meditate on it for as long as you can in the morning when you first wake up, before you get out of bed. Visit it anytime throughout your day when you have a few moments to let your mind enjoy a little vacation. Your commitment to living your Reality Plan will grow every time you do this JuicyFeel, and that commitment will draw in Universal assistance that will blow your mind. Watch for it, expect it, and act on it when prompted. One of my favorite Kafka quotes is: "God gives us the nuts, but he doesn't crack them." Accept those nuts with exhilarating gratitude, and get crackin'.

Additional JuicyFeel to Anchor Your Juicy Joy Reality Plan

— Move around, get into alpha, and imagine yourself as a guest on your favorite TV talk show. You look hot as hell.

— Imagine the host(s) interviewing you about this amazing life you've created for yourself. Give long and thoughtful answers to these talk-show questions:

- "How do you feel now that _____ [fill in the blank with the full fruition of your Juicy Joy Reality Plan]?"

- "What's your favorite part about all of this?"

- "How is your life different now?"

- "Tell us about a typical day in your exciting new life!"

- "What else has changed?"

- "Describe what it feels like to wake up every morning in this exceptional life you've created."

Write in your journal about how it felt to be on the talk show. If you felt embarrassed or worried about your answers, or wanted to deflect attention away from yourself, do it over and over until you can feel nothing but pride and excitement about sharing the details of your fabulousness. When you get to that point, study your mannerisms on the show, the way you're speaking, dressing, carrying yourself. Adopt this way of being as your new personal style. Go through your day, every day, as if you've just left the set of this talk show.

JuicyFeel Checkups for Your Reality Plan

You want to spend as much time immersed in the imaginary world of your Reality Plan as you possibly can. The more focus and attention you give it, the more speedily your outer reality will catch up with your inner reality. As you work with this JuicyFeel, an occasional hiccup or incongruity may surface. That's to be expected, so be thankful when it happens. Awareness leads to adjustment. Here are a few checkups you can do to make sure your efforts are as pure and effective as they can be. You'll find more at the Juicy Joy online community.

— This JuicyFeel should feel absolutely blissful. If you experience any uncomfortable little tugs while you're at it, pull out the specific desires and examine them one by one to see if they carry any unwanted baggage in your belief system.

For example, I intend to make an enormous contribution to the world as a personal-development author and teacher, but there was a time when I felt a tug about that in my Reality Plan. Upon close examination, I realized that I had underlying anxiety about the time-management aspect of such a grand goal. Would I have so many commitments and obligations that I wouldn't have time for my kids, for my friends, for a romantic relationship?

I recognized that I subconsciously associated success with being a *slave* to success. That little resistance was keeping me from stepping fully into my dream. All I had to do to remedy the glitch was to deliberately incorporate the energy of this additional component into my Reality Plan: My juicy, fulfilling career allows me ample time to pursue my passions (which mostly means learning new things involving my career anyway) and also leaves me plenty of free time for living my Juicy Joy—because I can't teach it if I don't take time to live it!

— Check in with yourself throughout your day and ask, *To the best of my ability, am I consistently acting as if my Juicy Joy Reality Plan were already a reality?*

If your goals are financial, for example, you need to be very appreciative and celebratory about whatever money you do currently posses or are in the process of earning. You cannot make the mistake of focusing on a lack of money. Is there anything you're spending money on right now that feels a little like a luxury? Do you berate yourself for this spending? If so, you're energetically keeping your financial goals out of your reach. It's imperative that you decide exactly what you plan to spend, and then, since you're spending it anyway, *enjoy* spending it! Love every second of it, and be grateful for the opportunity to make each purchase!

Make a list of nice things you own, or vacations you've taken, or anything you've used money for in the past. Really feel your appreciation for those things. Remember how you wanted them, and then bought them, and how much you enjoyed that moment. If you didn't enjoy that moment, rewrite it in your memory so that you did. Appreciation for whatever money you currently have and whatever money you've had in the past is the surest ticket to accruing more money in your future. If this is hard for you—if you have trouble feeling deep appreciation for the things you've bought in the past—then what makes you think that the things you want to buy in the future are going to make you any happier?

To get to the right feeling place around any particular issue, you might need to customize a special JuicyFeel for it. To continue with the money example, you might make a list of everything you'd buy if money were no object. What would you buy first? Imagine yourself writing that check or unfolding copious bills from your wallet, confident and joyful in your purchase. Imagine bringing that item home. What does it feel like to own it? Who would you show first? What specific kind of happiness would it bring you? Focus on your senses. What would you buy next? Spend some time going down the list, feeling each item fully. What would it feel like to have so much wealth? Where would you most like to be charitable? What would it feel like to write that check to your favorite charity?

This checkup can be customized for any area in your life where you feel a lack. If you're a workaholic, it might be a lack of *time* that trips you up. You'd need to make sure to fully enjoy and appreciate any time you do spend away from your work, and guard against the tendency to worry or feel guilty about taking that time for yourself.

— This is the most important checkup, so do this one weekly or even more frequently if you need to. Let yourself imagine the whole taco-load. Whatever you most want, see yourself having it in spades. Beyond your wildest dreams. Get to the feeling place of that. From your perspective while you're there, answer these questions in your journal, NakedWriting style:

- *What beliefs do I have about myself from this perspective of living my Reality Plan?*

- *What beliefs do I have about the world?*

- *What beliefs do I have about men/women?*

- *What beliefs do I have about money?*

- *What beliefs do I have about the Universe loving and assisting me?*

See if any other questions come to you that might pertain more specifically to your Reality Plan. How does it feel to answer those questions? Do the beliefs you listed while immersed in your Juicy Joy Reality Plan match your day-to-day, present-time beliefs? If not, it means you are not yet a vibrational match to your Plan, and you are unwittingly impeding its fruition. You must get yourself to authentically adopt the best beliefs now.

Make a list of facts that lend support to the beliefs you want to have. Gather as much evidence as you possibly can that the beliefs you have in your Juicy Joy Reality Plan are credible and worth adopting full-time. It is critical that you live your life as though your Reality Plan were already your reality. Speedy, phenomenal results depend less upon *what you're doing as they depend upon who you're being and what you're believing.*

Taco-Filling in a Juicy Nutshell

Taco-Filling is creating a vivid imaginary world to use as a blueprint for the real-life experiences you will soon be attracting. In this step, you allowed yourself to dream loudly. You opened your heart wide enough to rummage around in its cobwebby corners so you could pull out the desires of your most authentic core being.

Are you tingling with excitement over what's about to unfold for you? (If you're nodding your head, you get an A+.) Expect miracles. I'm feeling the need to say that again: *Expect miracles.* Your authentic expectation is truly all that is necessary to usher your wildest dreams into fruition.

If you're having trouble accessing that kind of genuine, honest expectation, I get it. It goes against so much of your early programming. That's why the JuicyFeels are so important. Every belief you've held throughout your lifetime has created neural pathways in your brain. They're real, physical features of your real, biological brain, and that's not easy to mess with.

But every time you focus all your attention on your JuicyFeels, you're creating *new* neural pathways—new physical brain bits. It may take some time to get these new creations as strong as the old ones, and your goal is to actually get them way stronger. So be kind and patient with yourself. Grab on to any glimmer of belief you can catch a glimpse of, and do all you can to magnify and enjoy it. After all, the technology of the subliminal messages embedded in the JuicyFeel audios has been proven effective in double-blind studies by independent researchers at leading universities. (If you need convincing, read about Eldon Taylor's scientifically verified, patented subliminal system at **InnerTalk.com**.)

The bottom line is this: Your belief in your JuicyFeels is what will ultimately turn them into powerful manifestation tools, but *you do not have to believe in them prior to using them.* Just start. Just start wherever you are and let the scrumptious energy of your JuicyFeels infect you little by little. Why would you ever want to resist something that feels so good?

Even if it's hard for you to believe, you *have* already made great strides toward living an abundant, love-filled life of Juicy Joy. So far, each of the steps to your glorious, gutsy self has been designed to help you get real—to help you uncover and fall in love with the parts of yourself you've denied or never even knew existed. That's where the juice lies, and it's the only route to living Juicy. You've arrived at the point in your journey where you're ready to look at getting real not only with yourself, but with others as well.

STEP SIX

GUT-DRIPPING

You can only be in authentic relationship with another to the extent that you are in authentic relationship with yourself. Now that you're enjoying a Juicy-Joyful love affair with preciously imperfect you, let's get that love flowing with the people in your life as well. Gut-Dripping is the art of loving yourself enough to take that true, authentic you out into the world for a test-drive. You might not choose to come from your rawest, most authentic core with every person in your life all the time, but in your most important relationships—the ones you count on to sustain you—it's an absolute must that you do.

The disturbing name of this step is deliberate because Gut-Dripping involves some stretching beyond your comfort zone. It's being prepared to open up, bare your soul, spill your guts, and be completely vulnerable when the situation warrants it, which is far more often than you'd think. Fulfilling relationships and genuine connections between humans cannot exist without Gut-Dripping.

You're going to be looking at all of your relationships—past, present, and future—through new eyes. You'll come to some new awarenesses about how your past relationships have shaped your present ones, and why your present relationships are full of valuable information about your current level of self-love. You'll learn powerful tools for attracting future relationships that are in perfect alignment with your new life of Juicy Joy.

Some personal-development plans stress how we need to meet all of our own needs for ourselves, and of course there's value in that, too. You don't ever want to feed off someone else's energy. But once you're living from your Juicy-Joyful authentic core, there's no danger of that. You'll be continually nourished by a natural abundance of life-force energy; plenty for your own personal needs. And then the human craving to share who you are with another person, to see that person and be deeply seen, and to have opportunities to give of yourself from that deep place—that's a definite and delicious component of a Juicy-Joyful life.

Do You Know How to Love and Be Loved?

It took me a long time to completely integrate the common pop-psych assertion that until you are generous and loving with yourself, you are incapable of loving anyone else. I paid lip service to that concept for many years before I was able to fully align my consciousness with its truth. This premise is a difficult one for many of us, but it's also an important one because feeling responsible for other people's happiness—or panicking at the thought of disappointing anyone in any way—is damaging to you *and* to everyone around you.

One of my all-time favorite teachers of authenticity and self-love is best-selling author Alan Cohen. I asked him to share some wisdom for this book, and he said, "Self-love, self-honoring, and self-care are absolute prerequisites to success and service. The more love you feel, the more love you have to give. World transformation begins with wholeness of heart."

There's no way around it—you have to love you first. It's time to discover where in your life you're being true to yourself, and where you might still be selling out your own Juicy Joy in order to get approval, respect, or some kind of outer-originated stroke. It's a tricky balance for most of us because the need for connection with others is so deeply embedded in our humanness. We falsely assume that being what others want us to be will foster this connection, when the opposite is actually true.

NakedWriting: Who Are You to Them?

You should be very familiar with Mirror You by now, even if you've been making changes and additions along the way. Call that best you vividly to mind—what you're doing, how you're being, how you speak and move and dance. Bask in those good feelings for a few moments.

Then, in your Juicy Joy journal, write down the top traits that really exemplify who you are as Mirror You. Yes, I know you've done it before. Do it again.

Now write down the names of five to ten people you spend the most time with. If you have kids who are still children, don't count them. Which *adults* do you have the most interaction with on a daily or weekly basis? If you spend a generous chunk of time and emotional investment on the phone with someone who lives far away, that person might make the list. Depending on your circumstances, list anywhere from five to ten adults, but make sure you include everyone you have any real emotional connection with.

Now look at the first name you wrote down, and imagine Mirror You having some sort of interaction with this person. If you were full-on exhibiting every trait you just attributed to Mirror You, how would this person be reacting to you? Does this imaginary scene feel like expansion in your body, or does it feel like contraction? You'll feel it if there's an energetic chasm. Jot down any thoughts.

Repeat that process with each person on your list. What you're really asking is: *How would this person feel or react if I became every bit of this best self I want to be, and I were fully exhibiting those traits I listed for myself?* Your gut response to that question lets you know if you believe that you can count on this person to support you in your blossoming.

Once you've made guesses as to which people would support you, draw a smiley face or frowny face next to their names, accordingly.

It's to be expected—and completely natural—for the people closest to us to prefer that we remain the same. Many people who love you will feel threatened by your commitment to a bigger, brighter version of you. It doesn't mean they're horrible people; it just means they're human. But since you are a tribal creature by nature, their resistance to your growth can be a significant energetic hindrance to it.

JuicyFeel to Test Your Guesses

— To test your guesses and get clarity on anyone you're unsure about, get yourself to alpha and think of the first person in question. Set the intention that you will be clear and honest and open to whatever naturally surfaces for you.

— Imagine this person sitting with you as you exist right now, in this present moment, while you tell him or her in great detail about Mirror You and your dedication to becoming that you. Tell this person, with all the authentic enthusiasm you naturally feel, all about your Juicy Joy journey and the life you are creating for yourself.

— Is it comfortable for you to imagine sharing your plans with this individual? How do you imagine the reaction?

— Jot down any insights in your journal, and repeat the Juicy-Feel with everyone on your list who needs further clarification.

If you feel any trepidation about declaring your Mirror You intentions to someone, it's probably due to an underlying fear that this person may not be able to support you in becoming that version of yourself. You don't need to judge anyone for that. If you really aren't sure what someone's reaction would be, I encourage you to have the conversation for real and find out.

Most of us have a number of relationships that are comfortable and enjoyable, but lack the depth of genuine connection. Sharing your innermost self with another is a meaningful compliment, and very often results in a richly satisfying deepening of the relationship. You may be surprised by how many of your friends are willing to connect on this level with you and share their own vulnerabilities and dreams once you open that door for them by sharing yours.

NakedWriting on Non-Supportive Relationships

For each person on your list who got a clear frowny face, answer these questions in your journal:

- What do you get from being in this relationship?

- Is there hope that this relationship can be adjusted so that you'd get the support you need to be your best self? Would it survive some newly defined boundaries?

- If setting new boundaries failed to change the nature of the relationship, would you be willing to end it or limit it? (In the early stages of being true to yourself and your highest joy, this may be the most difficult question.)

- When you think about ending this relationship, what fears come up?

- Do you feel obligated to this person?

- Are you feeling guilty at the thought of ending it? If you took guilt out of the equation, would you be happier without this relationship?

Are You Abusing Yourself Through Your Relationships?

If you're not already relating to everyone in your life as Mirror You (the true, authentic you) make a vow to yourself, right now, that you are going to start doing that. It might feel difficult at first, and you will likely meet with some resistance since the people in your life aren't used to you showing up that way. Try to give everyone the benefit of the doubt and go into each interaction expecting the very best. We all assume that others think about us much more than they actually do. Most people are too busy thinking about themselves to spend too much energy thinking about you. If you are resolute in your decision to behave as Mirror You from now on, it won't take the people in your life long to get used to it and begin treating you accordingly.

Have a discussion about it with the people who are closest to you. Let them know what's going on so they don't think you're just having a weird day. You might feel nervous about having the conversation, especially if it's the first time you're communicating in this raw, real way. The best thing to do if you're nervous is to just be honest about that. Anytime there's something that's hard to say, it's because you fear how it will be received. So set it up in advance.

Before you launch into it, say, "There's something I want to share with you. I'm afraid I won't come across the way you expect me to, because I've been making some changes. I'm nervous to talk about it . . ." I got that tip from one of my fabulous coaches, Christian Pankhurst. Christian says, "When you share the fear of sharing before what it is you actually want to share, it sets the other person up to be present, to connect, and sets the right stage for that person to receive you the way you desire."

Remember that your time and your attention are your most precious commodities. If you're giving a significant portion of your time to someone who is energetically holding you back from being your most authentic, fabulous self, it will naturally impede your progress. Every relationship we allow to exist in our lives provides insight into the way we are feeling about ourselves. If you allow anyone to abuse you in any way, to any extent, it's important to become very aware of that and look at why you allow it. With the exception of your own young children, every relationship is a choice. Feeding your precious energy into a relationship with someone who doesn't treat you well is making the choice to abuse yourself.

The good news is that regular maintenance of your Juicy Joy will make unsupportive relationships a thing of the past, since people who don't support you will naturally fall away. Their vibrational frequency will no longer match yours. They won't be pulled toward you, and you won't be pulled toward them. Once you are truly loving and honoring yourself, there will be no draw toward anyone who does not love and honor you to a similar extent.

NakedWriting: So *That* Explains It

In your Juicy Joy journal, make a list of the most prominent traits of the most significant person in your life right now. If you're married or in a romantic relationship, choose that partner. If not, choose your best friend or the person you spend the most time with. And don't sugarcoat it—we all have good and bad traits, so just list the top ones that come to mind, honestly, about this person.

You've no doubt heard the cheesy romantic line, "You complete me." Well, often, subconsciously, that's exactly why we choose our partners or friends. We feel, on a subconscious level, that they complete us. That's why it's often true that opposites attract.

Your partner's traits that you wrote down are probably the traits you wanted for yourself at the time you chose this person. Think back to who you were when you invited this person into your life. Can you see any ways in which you might have been hoping that he or she would complete you?

Keep in mind that sometimes a trait we originally admired about someone becomes exaggerated to an undesirable extreme over time, as our viewpoint shifts. If you once chose a partner whom you now perceive to be egocentric and self-absorbed, it doesn't mean that you wanted to be those things when you chose her, but it could mean that you suffered from too little self-esteem and were attracted to her seemingly booming confidence.

As you balance that trait within yourself, you could begin to perceive her "confidence" in a more negative light. As we discussed in the Judgment-Flipping chapter, there's a fine line between judging someone and admiring/envying her. See if you can draw any conclusions by scaling the various traits you've identified up or down.

If it's been a while since you chose this partner, look back and see how you ranked at that time on the predominant traits you listed for that person, versus how you rank on them now. Sometimes we subconsciously choose to spend just the right amount of time with someone for us to absorb what we need from them—the rub-off effect. Then, once we've achieved the balance we needed with that particular trait, the relationship becomes less important for our growth, and our evolving with this person is complete. In many cases, the primary reason two people are drawn together is for this kind of reciprocal growth opportunity, a symbiotic propelling of one another to new levels of consciousness.

When that aspect of evolving together is complete, one or both of the partners might be drawn to leave the relationship to find new opportunities for evolving, but that is not always the case. Many healthy relationships exist simply because the two people love each other, are vibrating at a similar level, and want to keep sharing themselves with one another. They have the same vision—the same definition for what a good relationship is. A healthy relationship could start out from that place, or it could become that way over time, after the balancing out of one another's traits has produced two fully whole and self-loving adults.

Secrets Block Love

Intimacy depends upon transparency. We all want to be seen, fully, by our partners and loved for who we are. But it's not up to our partners to make that happen. It's up to us to show up as our most transparent selves, and only when we're able to do that will we be capable of truly receiving love from anyone. When we hide bits of who we are, out of fear of being judged, we're energetically declaring that these parts of us are unlovable. Having that declaration in our filters then blocks us from being able to receive love, no matter how hard anyone tries to love us.

To varying degrees, we all keep secrets about actual events. But the easiest secrets to keep—the most rampant ones—are those concerning the way we feel about things. Sometimes we keep those secrets so tightly under wraps that we even keep them from ourselves. We tell ourselves that we feel one way (the socially acceptable way) when in reality, if we get very, very truthful with ourselves, we know that we feel a different way. Maybe it's a way that we're fearful to reveal because we're *judging ourselves* for it, and therefore expect others to judge us as well. But this fear blocks us from true intimacy and connection.

Here's a terribly extreme example of what I'm talking about. I was presenting this topic during a workshop a few years ago, and a participant asked if he could follow up with me privately afterward. I encouraged him to share whatever he had discovered about himself in the safe workshop environment I felt I had created—designed to free him from the judgments he held against himself and his fear of judgment from others. But he assured me that his case was significantly different, so I agreed to speak with him privately.

After the workshop, this lovely, sweet man who had endeared himself to everyone there confided to me that for many years, he had been harboring sexual fantasies about young children. He sobbed deeply with the release of this long, long-held secret. To compound the matter, he made his living as a physical-education teacher at a prominent private elementary school.

Henry told me that he had never acted on his fantasies, and I believed him. He assumed that I would be repulsed by him now. Even so, he said that I had made such a strong case for revealing our secret shame that he had been willing to endure his humiliation for the first time so that he could experience the release of his secret and find out if—as I had promised—doing so would lighten the pain and loneliness of his daily existence.

Did I recoil in horror? No. To the best of my memory, this is what I said to him: "Everything I've experienced about you and your energy during this class has led me to regard you as a kind, insightful, intelligent man who is dedicated to personal growth and to elevating his level of consciousness. The only revision I have now made to my original assessment of you is that you are also one of the bravest students I've ever had—and one that I have no doubt is ready to go the distance in creating a meaningful, purposeful life."

I asked Henry if he had ever talked with a therapist about his sexual fantasies. He admitted that he had known he should, but his shame had been too great. We talked about that being the first step for him, along with lots of self-forgiveness work. It wasn't an overnight process for Henry, but when I spoke with him a few months later, he had made so much progress with his therapist that I suggested the idea of him going more public with his issue. That, of course, was the opposite of what he felt compelled to do.

I asked him to consider how rampant, how unfathomably common, child sexual abuse is. The inclination he was feeling was hardly unusual, in spite of it being one of the most abhorrent and harshly judged crimes our culture suffers. What if all these people who were feeling those desires were to have a place to safely work through and transcend them? What if someone helped and comforted these monsters of society? Someone who understood firsthand, and was therefore able to see beyond the "monster" label?

What if such a person ran programs that let people with these feelings find community; programs based on the 12-step model, perhaps? Surely, if such a program existed, it would be responsible for saving countless children from experiencing this form of abuse. He could work with prisoners already convicted of these sorts of crimes. He could form some kind of ironclad, anonymous, online support system for those who—like him—were brave enough to seek help.

The possibilities for becoming a monumental force of good in the world are staggering for someone in his position. And they all start with one person forgiving himself, stepping fully into the totality of who he is, and finding a way to elevate the source of his shame into his most profound accomplishment. The simple fact is: there are obviously many people walking this earth who sexually desire young children. Henry was one of them. These facts, in and of themselves, are just facts. No one can change those facts by denying or harshly judging them. They're just what is. Henry got to choose what to do with this fact about himself.

So back to fear and love. Obviously, this secret Henry was keeping made true connection with anyone impossible. When he let more and more people know his secret, there were many, as he expected, who did recoil in horror. And it eventually cost him his job. However, it ultimately also led to the best, most peaceful, joyful, purposeful period of his life—where he did find friends (including a love partner of appropriate age!) who celebrated his bravery and commitment to his authenticity and to being the best person he could be. These people gave Henry the love and respect he had always longed for . . . and for the first time in his adult life, he was able to truly *receive* love. He could feel it and accept it because the enormous secret that had been blocking it was finally out of the way.

What far-less egregious secrets are you harboring that block you from experiencing true self-love and genuine connection with others? Take a moment to be still with that question, and write any insights in your journal. Is there anyone in your life you'd consider sharing these insights with?

What's Your Trigger?

Let your mind wander to your childhood for a moment. Imagine a situation where you felt judged by a parent. What is the first word that comes to mind to represent their judgment of you? How does this word feel now, when you think about it? Chances are you've spent much of your life trying to prove yourself to be the opposite of this word. But there's also a good chance that you secretly, subconsciously, fear that you do possess this trait. Look to see if that might be true for you, even if your first instinct is to deny it. If you feel any energy around this word—if it triggers some discomfort—then it's active for you, though you may not be aware of it.

For Lynn, the word was *selfish*. She was the oldest child, and her single mother expected Lynn to take care of her younger siblings when she went out on dates or out with her friends. If Lynn ever complained about missing opportunities to go out with her own friends, her mother would tell her what a selfish bitch she was. Lynn's mother loved her, but she was a highly dramatic and volatile person, and her loving style was to alternate between steamrolling Lynn with affection and raging at her when Lynn did anything to displease her. Lynn always felt that she had to be very careful not to set her mother off, and she established a pattern of tiptoeing through the land mines—a pattern she subconsciously brought with her into adulthood.

A child who has internalized a deep shame over being selfish is likely to become an adult who goes to great lengths to prove her unselfishness, especially when, as in Lynn's case, the consequences of being judged as selfish were so severe. Not surprisingly, Lynn became an anxiety-ridden pleaser, always desperate to prove how giving and selfless she was. But since deep down she had accepted her mother's assessment of her, she couldn't love herself—and she couldn't ever be authentic with the people in her life for fear that they'd discover her horrible "true" nature.

Since she was an overgiver, Lynn naturally attracted friends and lovers who were overtakers. When she did become involved with anyone who was generous and wanted to give love freely to her, she'd immediately become uncomfortable because too much receiving triggered her deeply embedded fear that she was, as her mother had so often declared, a "selfish bitch." On a conscious level she craved love, while unconsciously she pushed it away. All the negative energy Lynn was storing around the concept of selfishness had caused her to hate herself and try to hide *all* aspects of selfishness within her, even its scaled-back, healthy counterparts: self-love and self-respect.

Lynn had to do some work to understand that her mother's judgment had been nothing more than projected self-judgment, and actually had nothing to do with her. Lynn came to realize that her overgiving was not coming from a healthy, genuinely loving place, but from a terror that had gotten firmly lodged in her filter as a protective mechanism—one that may have served a valuable purpose in her childhood but was now causing dysfunction and resentment in her relationships. Lynn was able to dig up the deeply buried and denied piece of her that *was* actually self-honoring, and for the first time accept and love that part of her.

To help her become desensitized to the word, Lynn's classmates started affectionately calling her "Selfish Bitch" and encouraging her to behave selfishly in the class. The irony made it funny; the levity loosened up the crusty old patterns; and the game did wonders for Lynn's ability to step into her healthy, glorious, gutsy self.

Releasing a long-stored negative self-judgment will almost always result in ripple effects that clear up all kinds of seemingly unrelated negative beliefs as well. Going after that one worst thought you had about yourself just seems to automatically free up the energy around all the lesser ones.

JuicyFeel: Bring It into the Light

— Move your body, and relax into alpha brain-wave state. What's your word, or phrase, or hurtful feeling? What is the worst judgment you remember hearing from your parents? Or maybe the judgment that stands out most for you was from a sibling, friend, or teacher. You know you've found it when it triggers an inward cringe, an instinct to push it away. Call it forth instead. Bring it right up to your conscious attention. Some common ones are *stupid, incompetent, selfish, weak, insignificant, failure, unlovable,* and *something's wrong with you.* Sometimes it's more like a repeated impression than a memory of actual words being said.

— No matter who leveled this insult, can you see the truth behind it now? Can you see that it was this person's self-judgment projected onto you?

— Imagine the whole scene, as vividly as you can. Where were you? How old were you? If you don't remember a specific incident, make one up. Whatever you imagine right now will be more accurate than you think.

— Have you got the scene? Now go back to that magical movie theater where you're the protagonist and imagine that this whole scene is unfolding up on the screen.

— Be an all-knowing audience member for a moment. Does the audience buy into the insult? Or is it feeling love and sympathy for the child in this situation? Sit in this theater seat for a few minutes, feeling deep compassion for your child-self up there on the screen.

— Now imagine that a new character strides into the scene. It's Present-Day You, dressed exactly as you are dressed right now. Present-Day You is the child's ally. Yay! The audience is relieved!

— Present-Day You tells your insulter to never call Child You that again, and your insulter stomps off screen in a huff.

— Then Present-Day You gets down to eye level with Child You, and the camera zooms in for a big, warm hug.

— Up on the screen, in your own words, let Present-Day You comfort Child You and assure you that the insult has no bearing in reality. In language the child can understand, explain that the judgment was actually only about the one who leveled it.

— Sing Child You's praises, and promise that you'll always be here now to make sure Child You knows how intrinsically wonderful and special he or she is.

— Spend some time basking in the love energy before you leave this JuicyFeel.

Scale It Back to Balance It

Do you feel any loosening of the resistance around your trigger word from doing that JuicyFeel? You may need to repeat it several times to get to the deep feeling place where this wound can be unwound. If you still believe that the trigger word accurately applies to you in a negative way, it probably means that you've created some evidence in your life to support it. If that's the case, I want you to again consider that the *belief* you had about yourself—whether conscious or unconscious—is what led you to create the evidence. Allowing the belief to remain will only cause you to create more similar evidence. Working now to unwind the belief will lead you to create the opposite kind of evidence from this point forward.

Remember in the Judgment-Flipping Step, when we learned to scale back negative traits to find their positive counterparts? Try doing that now with your trigger word. In Lynn's example, she needed to find a positive, scaled-back version of selfishness that she could love and honor in herself. One way I helped her do so was by reminding her how many people would benefit from her becoming more self-honoring. She'd be a great model for her kids. She'd strengthen all her relationships by finally becoming transparent with her loved ones. She'd release others from feeling inadequate around her saintliness, and she'd give others the privilege of allowing them to give to her and know she was receiving their love.

The truth is that all human beings have aspects of themselves that are selfish. Once Lynn acknowledged that and stopped hating herself for it, she could consciously manage the degree to which she expressed that natural part of herself and make sure it was a degree that allowed her to strike a healthy, self-loving balance.

Can you come up with similar validating aspects of your trigger word, scaled back to its positive version? The idea is to stop resisting the trigger by recognizing it as a universal human trait you can balance and love within yourself. Once you've brought your trigger out into the light of conscious awareness and balanced it, you have forever released yourself from its negative energetic hold on you and its impact on your life.

If you have more than one trigger word or phrase from your childhood, go through the JuicyFeel with each of them. You didn't have a choice about what got lodged in your filter as a child, but you do now have a choice about what you allow to remain there. *There's no point in complaining about how badly you were treated if you continue today to treat yourself the same way.*

It's important to understand that your parents were acting from their own mucky filters, and probably had no way of knowing the affects their behaviors would have on you. Most parents believe they're doing the best for their children. Thank your parents for doing their best, whatever that happened to be.

What makes it so hard sometimes to accept and thank our parents is that we've absorbed many of their shadow traits. Or, as in the above example, our parents have projected their own shortcomings onto us, and we've internalized those judgments. We then subconsciously judge those traits in ourselves, which leads us to be overly sensitive to those particular traits in others. So we end up judging our parents for the very things they accused us of. See how cyclical it can get?

Think about how your trigger-word belief has played out in your life. How has that buried belief affected your relationships with others? Or, how has your determination to prove yourself the *opposite* of that deeply denied trait affected your relationships? Take a few moments to write your insights in your journal. Is there anyone in your life you'd consider sharing these realizations with?

Awareness Can Heal Harmful Childhood Relationship Patterns

Our childhood relationship patterns will always affect our adult relationships—that is, until we do the work to pull them out into the light and consciously rewire them.

Lila had been painfully shy as a child. She remembers her elementary-school teachers' frustration with her, and their constant demands that she "speak up" even when she felt that she was speaking as loudly as she possibly could. When she was given written work to do, her pencil marks on the paper were too faint to be read, again aggravating her teachers to no end. She stood apart from the other kids during free time, and was always last to be chosen for teams. Lila had absorbed a belief from her family that she was a burden to people, and the best way not to incur their wrath was to be as invisible as possible.

Noticing her unpopularity, her mother repeatedly told Lila that her classmates were all just jealous of her because she was so smart and pretty. Her mother meant well, but her words caused Lila to diminish herself even further in an attempt to be liked. As an adult student of Juicy Joy, Lila was finally able to understand the source of her self-deprecating patterns and do the reprogramming work necessary to unwind those childhood beliefs and step into her greatness.

Kevin is another valiant survivor of harmful childhood relationship patterns. Kevin's mom had hated his father with vitriolic vengeance, and whenever she wanted to wound or manipulate Kevin, she'd tell him, "You're just like your father." Since she made no bones about the fact that she despised her ex, what Kevin repeatedly absorbed throughout his childhood was that he was despicable and his mother loathed him. Kevin understandably had some challenges with self-love, which led to a difficult patch in his marriage.

Luckily for the relationship, Kevin's wife had opportunities to experience her mother-in-law's anger firsthand, so she understood the tragic circumstances that had shaped her husband's filter.

Since she had endured a highly dysfunctional upbringing as well, they were able to offer one another compassionate, mutual support, allowing them both to at last experience the stable, healing, unconditional love neither had been fortunate enough to have received in their childhoods.

Look Beneath the Surface

Another Juicy Joy student, Luisa, had never felt connected with her emotionally immature father. When her parents divorced, her younger siblings spent weekends with their dad, but Luisa was discouraged from joining them. Her mother told Luisa that the younger kids had to go because he paid child support for them, but since he refused to pay any for Luisa, she'd be better off to cut him out of her life completely.

Luisa was never given any explanation for why her father didn't pay child support for her, other than the obvious (to a child) reason—he had never loved her. Like Kevin's mother, Luisa's mom bitterly hated her ex and fed her daughter a steady diatribe about his many horrific shortcomings, even going so far as to try to get Luisa to join her in her prayers that he would be killed. In spite of her mother's assertions, Luisa felt a secret tenderness for her distant father, and immense confusion.

Many, many years later, when Luisa was in her 30s, she learned several things. The man she had known as her father was not her biological father. He had married her mother when Luisa was two years old, and a birth certificate had been forged so that Luisa would never be the wiser. Her biological father had never met her, but her mother had been married to another man when Luisa was born, and he had acted as her father for the first year of her life.

If you accept the psychological premise that our psyches are shaped by every circumstance we experience, even beginning in the womb, Luisa had been abandoned by three fathers by the time she reached adolescence. Some women would build up strong walls of defense from that paternal history, guarding themselves against romance and becoming openly distrustful of men in general. But every path is unique, and Luisa's dysfunction appeared to take a different direction.

She became obsessed with romantic love. She developed crushes that took on enormous energetic significance in her life, obliterating any other interests she might have developed. Her moment-to-moment happiness depended entirely upon the attention she was receiving or not receiving from the current object of her affection. Because she was so willing to do anything to attract and maintain relationships, she was able to line up a succession of monogamous partnerships throughout her teen and early-adult years. But none of them ever fulfilled her for long. The vacuum created by her unmet need for male love was too vast.

Because she harbored deeply entrenched feelings of not being lovable, Luisa never presented her authentic self in relationships. She was always so grateful to have a man's attention that she willingly became whatever he wanted her to be. Since sacrifice of that magnitude can never sustain a healthy relationship, Luisa would always become resentful over time, convinced that her partner didn't really love her.

Instead of becoming outwardly jaded about men and relationships, Luisa *appeared* to welcome them. The protective armor she'd built around her heart was less visible, but just as impenetrable. She knew the pain of loving freely and not having that love returned, so she'd unconsciously vowed never to expose herself to that kind of pain again. By never showing her lovers her full self, she never fully allowed them into her heart where they could hurt her. Because her pattern was unconscious, she didn't understand why her relationships never progressed to the deep level of intimacy she craved.

The truth is that Luisa *was* unlovable. No one could possibly love her, because she wasn't allowing them to. People can feel it when you are only offering them a portion of yourself. It might work to establish a short-term attraction, or a superficial relationship with an equally emotionally unavailable partner, but for genuine love to blossom, you must be willing to step out of the shadows. In order to be fully loved, you must first offer your full self up to *be* loved. And most of us can't bring ourselves to do that until *we're* loving *us*.

Relationship Pain Is Always an Opportunity to Examine Your Relationship to You

Think back to the last time you felt hurt or betrayed by some-one. What valuable message was the Universe sending you? Can you see how this incident was merely a reflection of your own judgments about *you?* Can you bring the underlying beliefs that birthed that situation out into the light now for self-healing?

Juicy Joy student Lori had a long history of people-pleasing and putting herself last, and she shared the following story during a workshop.

Lori's in-laws had been visiting her home for Christmas, and when they were packing to leave they asked if Lori would mail them the gifts they'd received. My student cheerfully assured them she'd mail the small pile, even though most of the items—such as gift cards, a scarf, and lotion—could have easily been packed in their luggage.

Lori packed up the items and brought them to the post office, along with the address of the new community her in-laws had moved into. She sent the package off and forgot about it. A week later, Lori's father-in-law sent her an e-mail asking about the pack-age. Lori told him she'd sent it and it would probably arrive any day. A few days later she got another e-mail from him, asking her to track the package. Lori had lost the receipt, which annoyed her father-in-law. He was certain Lori had written the wrong address on the label.

A few weeks later the package had still not arrived, and Lori's father-in-law was clearly angry with her. This woman felt terrible, and offered to replace everything that was in the package and try sending it again. Her father-in-law agreed that was what she need-ed to do. To the best of her ability, Lori repurchased the items, and she wrote a check well beyond what was needed to cover the cost of the things she couldn't replace.

She packed it all up again, and this time brought it to an alternate parcel-delivery service, determined that she'd buy insurance and make sure that the package could be traced at all times. She gave the clerk the address, and after a long search he informed her that the address did not exist in the United States postal system. They found a way to mail the gifts, but he explained that the first package could not have been delivered by U.S. mail because the community Lori's in-laws had recently moved into was so new that it was not yet recognized by the post office. Lori was relieved to be able to explain the solved mystery to her father-in-law, but he was dismissive and unapologetic.

Although the man did return a portion of the money Lori had sent, she was visibly distraught about his anger toward her. She wanted him to forgive her. She was so invested in being liked by her in-laws that she was blind to the way she was allowing them to mistreat her. In an attempt to open her eyes, some of her classmates suggested that it was Lori who should be mad at her father-in-law. But I pointed out that he had not been the one to suggest Lori replace the gifts. All he had done was angrily judge her.

As we know, any judgment of another is actually self-judgment. In this case, most likely it was the father-in-law's own fears of ever appearing incompetent that made him so harshly critical of Lori's seeming incompetence. Lori *could* have chosen to respond to his anger in a self-respecting, self-loving manner. It was she who had internalized and validated his judgment of her by offering to replace the gifts. He was not responsible for her reaction; he was simply having his own. His judgments of her could never have hurt her so deeply if she had not, on some level, agreed with them.

The jewel in the experience was the opportunity for Lori to clearly see how routinely she was failing to love and protect herself. It was beautiful to watch her progress as this new clarity jump-started her journey into a self-respecting, self-adoring woman. She was eventually even able to get in touch with some healthy awareness about her husband, who had watched the whole ordeal unfold without stepping in to defend or support her. What had felt like a terrible experience while she was going through it was truly a rich gift from the Universe in terms of helping Lori wake up to the changes she needed to make toward her Juicy Joy.

Other people will always respond to us in a manner consistent with our own self-appraisal. Lori had led her in-laws (and her husband) to feel entitled to treat her with disrespect, but they were only mirroring my student's feelings about herself. When she realized all the ways she'd been inviting disrespect from others, she got busy rewriting some laws that reflected her new self-image.

Have you noticed a pattern in all of these relationship stories? The Universe is capable of sending us many messages through our relationships, but by far the most common message is something to the effect that you are not honoring and loving yourself nearly as much as the Universe would like you to. Almost every hurt or upset you've had in relationships has been to alert you to this critical message.

What Self-Love Looks Like

Sandy was a regular at my Juicy Joy workshops, and she and I became friends. She was in love with Mitch, and it seemed that he loved her, too. But Sandy felt that he wasn't there for her to the degree she'd like. They lived several hours apart, and my friend did most of the driving to participate in his world. She was active in the spiritual community and wished that Mitch would accompany her to more of her events. They both were devoted to personal growth, which was wonderful for the relationship . . . but occasionally Mitch's path would lead him to need time away from Sandy to retreat to his man cave to work on himself and figure out what he wanted. She never complained about these interludes, always supporting him in his decisions and greeting him with open arms when he resurfaced.

Sandy was good at self-love, but we are all works in progress, no matter how evolved we become. For a while she was proud of the way she dealt with her disappointments about Mitch. But it was a truly beautiful day when her self-love finally outweighed her love for her man. I got chills when she called to tell me she had come to the conclusion that she deserved a relationship that met more of her needs. She wasn't whiny. She wasn't blaming Mitch. She had simply and calmly recognized her worth, and was ready to take the necessary steps to find a partnership that more closely matched her own personal definition of a good couple.

She told Mitch that she loved him, respected him for who he is, and wished him all the best, but she needed to end the relationship because—and these were her exact words to him—"I want more love than this. I want someone who knows he wants to be with me and is sure about that every day. I want someone who tells me he loves me every day; who misses me when he's not with me. I love you, but I'm not getting from you the kind of love I want to experience."

There was nothing open-ended in what Sandy was saying. She wasn't trying to solicit any kind of a reaction from him; she wasn't punishing him or trying to make him wrong. She was just authentically, lovingly expressing her reasons for ending the relationship. She truly believed that would be her last conversation with Mitch, and she was at peace with that.

But that's not how the story ended.

Mitch listened to Sandy. And seeing her that clear, in her self-loving, caused something to shift inside of him. His resistance melted away, and he professed his love for her with a depth and rawness she'd never seen in him. Their relationship changed dramatically after that conversation. Mitch became more vulnerable, more affectionate, more demonstrative of his love than he'd ever before allowed himself to be. It was a stretch for him, but it was the stretch he needed because he truly did love her, and it was only his fears that had kept him from the full expression of that love.

Now he's moved closer to where Sandy lives, attends many of her functions, tells her how much he loves her every day, and they're talking about getting married. Sandy was fully prepared to move forward in her life without Mitch, and that would have been an equally successful outcome.

On the surface, my friend's story resembles the ultimatum scenario common to less-conscious romantic partnerships. But it's actually the exact opposite. Relationship ultimatums are born out of a power struggle between the partners. There is no real love in unions where each partner is trying to manipulate and gain control over the other. Sandy wasn't trying to control Mitch or change him. She had simply gotten clear about the kind of relationship she wanted, and she was unequivocal in her knowing that she deserved to have it. Not every self-loving woman would want the exact things Sandy wanted, but she had a right to decide for herself what a wonderful partnership meant to her. Getting clear on what she wanted demonstrated true authenticity. Having the courage to hold out for it demonstrated true self-love.

Nothing is sexier to a potential romantic partner, man or woman, than a deeply self-loving person. Once Mitch saw Sandy the way she had started to see herself, he fell more in love with her than ever. Even though he still felt remnants of his old issues and commitment fears, his desire to keep her at all costs helped him rise above them.

Intimacy Is a Two-Way Street

When you've felt very close to someone, you've probably had the feeling that "I can be myself with her." It's a curious phrase, because there is no way that any person can actually prohibit you from being yourself. You can always make the choice to be yourself; there are just certain people who make it easier for you, by giving you a sense that they will not judge you. Releasing your judgments of yourself bolsters your immunity to judgments from others, and allows you to "be yourself" much more often.

The more transparent we become, the more we invite others to be transparent with us. Since all individuals have a deep yearning, buried beneath their fears, to break free of facades and live as their most authentic selves, most of us are irresistibly drawn to transparent people! We believe we're more likable when we hide our shadow parts, when in reality the exact opposite is true.

Here's a funny example. My friend Peter, who apparently likes to use Facebook as an internet dating site, posted the following on his profile as his "About You" information:

Hmm . . . Let's try this:

Insecure, sensitive Pisces (I cry after sex . . . probably from the mace).

Misunderstood, frustrated genius who hides behind humor to cover the sadness I feel inside.

Want that in your life?

Filthy, cruel, mean, insecure . . . and those are my good points!

I own an ad agency, play keyboards in a classic rock and blues band, do stand-up comedy, and host two radio shows! Effin' busy, but having the most fun of my life not workin' for "the man"!

Admit it—don't you love him? We all have parts of us that are filthy, cruel, mean, and insecure. When I see someone fully owning and embracing those aspects of himself, especially through humor, it actually makes me feel better about him! It gives me a sense that he must have those things in balance or he wouldn't be putting them out there. Don't you feel like he'd be fun to hang out with? Don't you feel like you'd be free to be your most authentic self with him?

For intimacy to exist between two people, each half of the partnership needs to be committed to a full-on effort at personal transparency. Showing up in your relationship as transparent as you possibly can is the first and most important step. You can never demand transparency *from* your beloved, nor will you ever have any ultimate control over another's capacity for transparency. But as a loving partner, you *can* and *must* create a sacred, welcoming space for it. Our fears of intimacy are usually rooted in concerns about sharing of ourselves, but an equally critical component of the intimate relationship is the desire and determination to deeply *see* your partner, no matter the extent to which that person is currently capable of authentic sharing.

It's a fairly accurate stereotype that men often find it more difficult to share deeply of themselves than women do. I don't believe it's a genetic flaw, or that they're purposefully holding out. When we enter the Earth experience, we're all pretty much wired for full-on authenticity, but then our upbringing takes its toll. In our culture, it's unfortunately common for men to be judged more harshly for displaying their emotions than women are. Expectations regarding emotional expression are just not as narrowly defined for us women as they are for our dudes.

It doesn't mean that guys are not as authentic; it just means that they may not be as skillful at accessing the full spectrum of themselves. (I think that's why men are so drawn to do Juicy Joy work; it helps them build those skills.) If you're a woman—or a guy who digs guys—reading this, know that your transparency is the greatest gift you can give your man, and it's the thing that will most powerfully allow him to inch toward his own. When he does let his guard down and begin sharing his hidden bits, you must be sensitive, compassionate, and respectful of how hard it can be for a man to reveal his soft underbelly.

A common trap a woman might fall into, particularly if her dude is the more reserved type, is to project all of her dream-guy emotional qualities onto her real-life man in a twisted fantasy where, underneath it all, he must really be these things. Since he's not showing her a lot of himself, he becomes like a clean slate to her, and she does her own filling in of the blanks. This obviously sets her up for disappointment, makes it even harder for him to be authentic with her, and powerfully works against true intimacy.

But while it's wrong to paint imaginary traits on your man, it's absolutely *right* to ferret out all the fabulous qualities he *does* posses, and make a point of praising and adoring them. Even better if you can find it in your heart to praise and adore a few of his less-fabulous traits as well—his quirky bits that might annoy others, but that you genuinely understand or find endearing. The more you can offer him this comfort level, the more free he'll feel to be himself with you. And you'll be modeling behavior that he'll hopefully emulate. Isn't being seen and adored for our whole selves what every one of us—man or woman—truly longs for in a romantic partnership?

The best relationships provide springboards for each person to evolve to ever-increasing levels of self-awareness and Juicy Joy. Knowing that your beloved cherishes and unconditionally loves every last speck of you creates an ironclad safety net for the fullest expression of your gifts and talents and efforts to become your biggest, brightest self. Providing that kind of security for your partner allows him the freedom to embrace his biggest destiny as well. Without imposing your own agenda, don't be afraid to authentically see more in him than he might be currently seeing in himself. The opportunity to see himself through your eyes will help him step into his true greatness. He is a divine being, as are you, and may need reminding of that.

This holds true for all of your relationships, not only your romantic ones. Seeing, appreciating, and celebrating the greatness in your kids, your friends, your employees, or your family members will always propel them toward their highest potential. If you're in a place of discord with someone, try to remember a time when that person was truly authentic and vulnerable with you or said something that touched you deeply. Vividly recalling and meditating on that memory will open the energetic connection between you and make it much easier for you to resolve the current difficulty.

Strand-Snipping

I believe that sharing your full transparent self with another who is also committed to full transparency must be the most exciting, fulfilling, freeing experience available to human beings. I believe the longing for that experience is hardwired in each of us, though for many people it's buried too deep beneath their web of fears to be consciously felt.

The degree to which your romantic relationship will succeed depends in great part on the degree to which you and your lover are matched on the issue of transparency. It's not uncommon for people operating at a similar level of emotional availability to be drawn together, only to find years later that one partner has stretched to a much greater capacity for transparency, while the other partner has remained the same.

It's painful to be in a relationship with someone you love who is not interested in seeing you as fully as you want to be seen, and is not capable of allowing you to see all of him or her. It's mostly fears and lack of self-love that keep people stuck at lower levels of transparency and emotional availability. And again, without love for self, it's not really possible to love another. Since all judgment is really self-judgment, individuals who lack self-love tend to be highly critical of others, especially their intimate partners.

My friend Christian Pankhurst uses a spaghetti-strand analogy to describe what happens in such relationships. He says that when we fall in love with someone, we create energetic spaghetti strands that connect our hearts. Every time one person belittles the other, makes a snide comment, or in some way causes pain to the other, it's like snipping a strand of spaghetti. Some greater betrayals may even cause whole clumps to be cut at once. You can do things to replace the snipped spaghetti with new strands as long as at least one of the original strands is in place. But once that last strand is cut, it's too late to rebuild. The relationship is over.

To keep your spaghetti strands intact, make every effort to deeply see and understand your partner, especially in times of judgment or conflict. Listen to comprehend, not to plan your next retort. Never assume that you know what your partner is thinking. Always ask. Repeat your interpretation back to be sure you've understood correctly. Then deeply trust that it's true, or talk it out until you can authentically feel that trust.

It's important to keep in mind that your partner is not against you, he's just *for himself,* so his approach is naturally going to be from his own perspective. You can maintain a different perspective and still try to understand him. Sometimes we're afraid to say, "I understand," because we think that implies agreement. Understanding is not agreeing; it's simply recognizing the validity of the other's experience. Make sure your ultimate intention is not just for you to get what you need, but for you *both* to get some of what you need.

JuicyFeel for Romantic Intimacy

This JuicyFeel will help you establish a deeply intimate connection with a lover, whether you already have someone in your life or not. It's best to listen to it on audio so you can pay full attention to your feelings.

— Start by entering your Mirror You JuicyFeel (which should be exceptionally easy for you to slip into by now). Let Mirror You wear something sexy this time, and spend a few moments getting pumped with the full-on recognition of your own wonderfulness.

— In your completely private, lush, natural setting, spread a soft blanket on the ground and relax on the blanket, knowing that your ideal lover is about to join you. You're so excited, thinking about how much you thrill each other, feeling the rich energetic connection between you even when you're not physically together. Relish the waiting, deliberately amping up your anticipation until the scrumptious tingle of sexual chemistry fills your whole body.

— Imagine your lover approaching. If you already have a real-life partner whom you want to increase intimacy with, imagine that person. If not, focus on the *feeling* of your lover's energetic presence instead of trying to visualize any physical features.

— Embrace your lover whichever way feels best in your imagination. Breathe in your lover's essence. Feel the electricity of your lover's skin against yours. Sigh deeply. You are home.

— Your lover has brought you a gift—the perfect gift that demonstrates a profound understanding of who you authentically are and what would most please you.

— Accept this gift and allow yourself to be swept away with the flood of appreciation you feel for this person who sees you so clearly. Passionately express your appreciation, in whatever sensual manner feels best to you. Taste God in your beloved.

— Wrapped in your lover's arms, recognize how utterly free and alive you feel. You could do or say anything at all in this moment, knowing that this person cherishes you, is irresistibly drawn to you, is curious about you, and is eager to witness the ever-evolving, full spectrum of your you-ness. You feel the same exhilarating intrigue about your beloved, and every moment you spend together offers thrilling new aspects of one another to explore.

— Your lover gazes adoringly into your eyes and whispers words to you—the perfect words you've always longed to hear.

— You share a final, soul-igniting embrace, and your lover leaves, having been inspired to go do something exquisitely meaningful for you that again demonstrates a poignant understanding of your most uniquely authentic desires.

— Blissed-out on the blanket, you bask in the joy and appreciation of having this amazing person in your life. You now know the love you've always dreamed of is possible. You can't stop smiling.

— While you're still immersed in the yummy juice of this Juicy-Feel, take a moment to answer these questions in your journal:

• What was the gift your lover brought you?

• What were the words your lover whispered to you?

• What did your lover leave to do for you?

The Truth about Your Ideal Lover

If you don't know what I'm going to say next, you haven't been paying attention. What's the prerequisite for having the kind of Juicy-Joyful love relationship you just imagined? In order to love anyone else, you must first do what? Say it with me: *You must first love yourself.* And to have big, big love in your life, you have to love yourself in a big, big way. Now that your subconscious has told you what the perfect gift for you would be, what the most perfect words you could ever hear would be, and what you'd most like done for you . . . guess who needs to take care of those things?

You do. To attract your ideal lover, you need to *become* your ideal lover. Go buy yourself that gift. Add those words to your mirror writings, and say them to yourself daily. Whatever you're waiting for a lover to do for you, go do it. Do all of these things for yourself in the spirit of big, big love—for you! Not because you aren't going to get the real-life lover, but because the best way to attract that kind of relationship is to treat yourself, right now, the way you most want to be treated.

The point I'm making here is *not* that you should do those things for yourself so that you won't need the lover after all. You won't find that in *my* book! I am a card-carrying believer that big, big love is your birthright—it's available to anyone who's willing to hold out for it and do the self-love work necessary to pull it in. The point is that everything in your life, most especially your romantic relationship, is providing a crystal-clear snapshot of how you're feeling about *you*. If you're in a lukewarm relationship, you have a lukewarm relationship with *you*. If you're in a horribly unfulfilling relationship, you have a lot of work to do—on loving *yourself*. To my mind, the promise of the possibility for big, big love is the very most compelling reason to get serious about your authenticity and self-adoration.

You know by now that the best way to bring in anything you want is to feel grateful for it in advance. In the first and last parts of the JuicyFeel you just did, your lover wasn't there, but you still felt the juice of the connection, didn't you? To find big, big love, just tap into *that* juice as often as you can. No matter what you're doing, vividly pretend that your yummy lover is already a solid fixture in your life. Pretend that he just ran to the store for milk. Relish the connection *before* a real-life ideal lover appears, and the Universe will have no choice but to bring you one. Read Arielle Ford's *The Soulmate Secret* for lots of ways to do that.

As I told Arielle, I used to think that I had self-love in the bag, but when I started imagining already having my ideal lover and getting glimpses of me through his eyes, it propelled my capacity for self-love into a whole juicy-new realm!

~

I was recently co-hosting a radio show when a listener called in with an intriguing situation. She had made a spirit connection with a deceased famous actor and believed that she had at long last found her soul mate. She described how in love they were, how strongly she felt his presence, and how happy their union made her. Determined to disprove the caller's fantasy, my co-host asked if she had orgasms with her spirit friend. The caller assured us that she did.

I asked her if they were exclusive, or if she'd consider dating a presently alive person. She replied that she would date a living person because she believed that her spirit lover could manifest as a "walk-in" at any time. When this happened, she explained, he would not remember their cross-dimensional relationship, but they'd recognize one another as soul mates.

Bingo! To my co-host's dismay, I told our caller to keep doing everything she was doing. She had found a unique way to *act as if* the perfect love she wanted were already a reality, so I knew she was vibrating at the right frequency to speedily draw such a love to her. When the caller hung up, my endearingly jaded co-host asked if I actually believed that she was having a relationship with the dead actor. "Who cares?" was my answer. I had no idea whether or not that kind of thing was possible, but it didn't matter. What mattered was that our crazy (or not) caller was in a juicy-receptive state for real love to find her.

Did you pick up on my implied suggestion with the details I shared about our caller's cross-dimensional love affair? Do *whatever works* for you to get as unabashedly vivid as you possibly can when you imagine how you want to feel with your partner. Again, it's your own imagination, so why would you scrimp on the juice? The more lusciously decadent and thrilling you can make this JuicyFeel, the more time you'll want to spend with it, and the more successful you'll be at raising your vibration to attract big, big love.

Beware the Sneaky Return of Old Relationship Patterns

Being a people-pleaser is like being an alcoholic—you don't ever consider yourself fully recovered; you just congratulate yourself for keeping it under control. Uh-hum (clearing throat). "Hi. I'm Lisa, and it's been 48 days since I did something to try to make someone like me." (Usually, it's more like 48 hours.) The default setting to people-please will always be there, but when you stay aware of it, you can deliberately make choices that honor your dedication to ever-evolving self-love and authenticity.

I was less than a week away from the deadline on this book, and I really wanted to make sure that it would be life changing for people. Maybe I also really wanted to impress Hay House. All I could think about, from daybreak to the wee hours of the night, was new ways to edit, tweak, and obsess. I was filled with excited energy and focus, planning to dedicate every remaining hour to creating a perfectly tweaked product I'd be thrilled to send in. I was used to juggling kid responsibilities and family obligations with my work, but somehow during those final writing days, the demands on my time from others seemed to quadruple.

All kinds of extra events with my kids popped up. My mother and grandmother had additional errands for me to run for them beyond our regular weekly grocery-shopping outing. My sister, whom I adore, moved into a home in my neighborhood, which thrilled me to no end. But the moving day took place during this precious final writing period, and of course I wanted to help her as much as I possibly could, as well as take my toddler niece off her hands so she and her husband could unpack. A dear friend announced a must-attend birthday gathering. I started feeling increasingly anxious as the hours I'd be away from my manuscript mounted. I felt my energy and vitality collapsing into that very familiar sensation of being powerless to get my own needs met because of the seemingly relentless needs of others.

Then I caught myself. How unconscious could I be? Here I am, writing about the importance of self-love and bragging about how I'd overcome my people-pleaser ways, and *I was still getting sucked into my old familiar patterns*. Duh! Instead of beating myself up (okay, I beat myself up for just a quick second), I took control. I lovingly expressed to the people in my life that this book was uber-important to me and every hour leading up to its deadline had become an exceedingly precious commodity. I asked for their understanding and support.

Greg took over with the kids. My mom and grandmother generously waived their right to my services that week. My sister's move was successful and harmonious with only one day's assistance from me. My friends understood and excused my absence. It was the perfect opportunity to tell people precisely how I needed their love, and then *allow* them to love me. They did it freely, happily, and without reservation.

I wish I didn't have to confess this to you, but it was still really hard and it still put me in a funk. The Universe was giving me a clear message that I'm not quite there yet when it comes to making self-honoring requests without worrying about how they'll be interpreted. *They* were fine with it. *I* wasn't. It would be nice if I could clone myself, but since I can't, I'm okay with this being my practice. Every day I get better at trusting that my self-love serves not only me, but my relationships and those I'm in relationship with as well. Every day I get more comfortable in my juicy self-loving. And I have to just keep loving myself for that.

Gut-Dripping in a Juicy Nutshell

Your relationship with yourself is the most important relationship you'll ever have, but since you are a tribal creature by virtue of your humanness, your Juicy Joy will depend, in large part, upon your relationships with others as well. Gut-Dripping is the art of loving yourself enough to present your most authentic self in your interactions with people.

Transparency is the key to the kinds of deeply connected relationships that characterize a Juicy-Joyful life. In this step, you uncovered some insights about the people in your present circumstances and which ones will be most supportive as you continue to grow into your most authentic and wonderful you. You examined your past relationships for clues as to what might be holding you back from living as your most real, Juicy-Joyful self. You read about the impediments to transparency that several Juicy Joy students overcame, and you probably saw in their stories some similarities to your own.

Your enjoyment of your relationships ultimately comes down to a series of moment-by-moment choices. Every moment in which you are relating to another person is a new opportunity to choose. You can choose to come from the position of judgment so that you can triumph and be right, or you can simply choose the position of empathy, connectedness, and gratitude for whatever lessons the interaction might bring. Pulling that decision-making process up into the light of your conscious awareness is the secret to Juicy-Joyful relationships.

Do you feel confident about your ability to now attract the kinds of authentic, deeply satisfying relationships you've always craved? Remember that your dedication to *your* transparency is what will most enticingly invite others to share their own truest selves with you. Morphing into what you believe others want you to be will always result in a vague sense of disconnect between you. It creates walls in your relationships that cause them to dry out, no matter how juicy they may have once seemed.

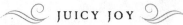

When you love yourself fully and completely, you naturally want to share that true you with the people around you. You feel the God-presence within you, and you can't help but recognize that God-presence in others. The next step, God-Dipping, will help to solidify that recognition for you, and ensure that all your relationships glide on the crest of that juicy, juicy wave.

GOD-DIPPING

You've come a long way, my juicy friend. But to keep living juicy, you need more than the right attitude—you need the right *altitude* as well. This final step is about getting up on the balcony so that you can view your journey, as well as the journey that lies ahead, from a higher perspective. This perspective will give you consistent access to your connection with Source, no matter what you've been calling it—God, the Universe, or just your own subconscious or Higher Self. Being able to dip into this connection whenever you need it will absolutely assure the continued expansion of your Juicy Joy and your ability to feel the God-presence in *you*.

A lot of the work you've done has focused on bringing the things you want into your life. It's time to step back from that just enough to realize that the point of that aspect of your Juicy Joy training has been simply to awaken you to the fact that you *have* that kind of manifestation power within you. It's a for-real, exciting piece of your true, authentic self!

The things you want will fluctuate perpetually—that's why you have an open-shell taco. Knowing that you can create whatever you want makes the *wanting* itself Juicy Joyful. Your happiness has never really depended upon your getting the specific things you believe you want, because once you have them, you'll just want something else. Your happiness depends on your deep understanding that your authentic *feeling* of already having those things is the key to pulling them in.

Ah, *feeling*. Have I convinced you that your feelings are far more powerful, far more significant, and far more authentically *you* than your thoughts ever could be? As my friend Tej Steiner, founder of the Heart Circle facilitating method, says, "You are not who you think you are. You are who you are when you stop thinking." So true, Tej!

A common thread within every major religion is quieting the mind so we can feel the divine within us. Western religions often stress prayer and repetition of specific liturgies. Eastern and Islamic religions all incorporate some form of meditation practice. Buddhism in particular stresses trusting feeling over thought. And in the Quaker tradition, they talk about "leadings" or "being called" to do something. The commitment Quakers make is to listen to this inner guidance and have the courage to follow it, even when they meet with external resistance.

According to master spiritual teacher Eckhart Tolle:

> You are cut off from Being as long as your mind takes up all your attention. When this happens—and it happens continuously for most people—you are not in your body. The mind absorbs all your consciousness and transforms it into mind stuff. You cannot stop thinking. Compulsive thinking has become a collective disease. Your whole sense of who you are is then derived from mind activity. Your identity, as it is no longer rooted in Being, becomes a vulnerable and ever-needy mental construct, which creates fear as the predominant underlying emotion. The one thing that truly matters is then missing from your life: awareness of your deeper self—your invisible and indestructible reality.

My Favorite Tool for Treating the "Collective Disease" of "Compulsive Thinking"

I've forever been enchanted by Tonglin meditation, and there are many forms of this ancient practice. I'm going to give you instructions for two Juicy Joy versions of my favorite application of it. Both would be handy to carry around with you, so consider downloading the free audios at the Juicy Joy online community.

If you've practiced yoga or dabbled with meditation, you've probably been taught the relaxation technique of breathing in peace and tranquility, and breathing out stress and negativity. It's really common . . . and you can forget it now. Tonglin meditation is the opposite of that.

It's from the *Tibetan Book of Living and Dying*, so it's Buddhist based. And Buddhists are all about *Namaste*—recognizing the divine in every person. "We are all one" is the big point with Buddhists. So from a Buddhist perspective, breathing fear and stress and anger and all kinds of emotional toxins out into the universe is kind of an unfriendly, karmically irresponsible thing to do. When we practice Tonglin, we take responsibility for our negative emotions without resisting them. We acknowledge that through nonjudgmental observation of them, the infinite power of the God-self within us can effortlessly transmute the energy of these emotions into pure divine awareness and love.

Here's how to do the quickie version:

- When anything comes up in your life that causes a negative charge in you, imagine it as a foul vapor —because we always perceive that these things are outside of us, right? Make the vapor as grimy, dark, hot, smoky, and horrific as the situation warrants.

- Now, consciously breathe *in* this cloud of negativity. This will seem super-counterintuitive at first!

- Swirl the cloud around and through your heart center, and feel the powerful alchemy of the divine, loving presence within you.

- When you breathe out, imagine your exhale as a blessing—a stream of pure, clear, loving light.

When you use this technique to address routine upsets in the midst of your busy day, that's about all you'll have time for. But you'll fall in love with Tonglin's magic and want to also practice the more leisurely version:

- To prepare for a full Tonglin meditation session, find a comfortable place where you won't be disturbed, and quiet your mind by relaxing and breathing into your heart with the intention of opening it.

- When you feel the stillness, just allow yourself to fully experience whatever pain, hurt, confusion, or sadness is there. Invite it without forcing it, and just remain open to whatever comes up for you.

- Imagine that foul vapor in front of you, and let it represent your negative emotions.

- Intensify the feeling, intentionally taking on all the pain of everyone in your family, your community, and the planet who might be suffering any kind of similar difficulty.

- Breathe it in, swirling this enormous burden through your heart-center, and observe how effortlessly you can transmute it.

- On the out-breath, send powerful waves of love and light to yourself and all people.

Know that you are making a difference in the world when you do this kind of energy work, because you truly are. And of course, what you give, you get, so doing Tonglin for the world actually intensifies your own healing. It puts you in the realm of "Big Mind" and frees you from getting caught up in your own isolated stuff. You move into connection with all people sharing similar pain, and in this way you realize that what you're facing is part and parcel of the human experience. Giving regular attention to the awesome magnitude of the divine power within you will strengthen your self-love muscle like nothing else!

Install the Namaste Lens in Your Filter

I have the Sanskrit symbol for Namaste tattooed on my right hip. Not the kind of tattoo that only lasts through a few showers and a good long swim. The *I-let-them-stick-needles-in-me* kind. I love that sweet little tattoo and the forever reminder of how sacred the concept of Namaste is to me. The final, critically important upgrade you must make to your filter is to snugly weave the Namaste Lens into it.

We hear about the power of gratitude all the time, but how many of us practice gratitude as often as we could? To me, the Namaste Lens is the answer. Simply put, Namaste means: The divine in me recognizes and honors the divine in you. It's the connection thing I've talked about throughout this book. It's the ultimate God-Dipping practice because it's waking up to the divine God-Love energy that runs through us all, connecting us in sacred and indisputable ways.

At the God-Dipping level of Juicy Joy, it's easy to truly love and honor all people with all their limitations. It's only our fears and protections that keep us from allowing ourselves to feel that love. This assertion is just an extension of the forgiveness work we did in the Story-Stripping chapter. You've probably heard the classic analogy about how holding a grudge against someone is like eating poison and expecting the other person to die, in that it harms the holder of the grudge far worse than the person the grudge is against.

In a similar vein, your soul-self wants to love everybody. It feels good to love. It doesn't feel good to judge and dislike people. Loving everyone doesn't mean you have to be in relationships with everyone. You can be honest with the people in your life regarding how much time you want to spend with them and what you want the nature of your relationship to be, while still loving every one of them.

Make one last list of the important people in your life—your favorite and your not-so-favorite ones. Look at them all through your Namaste Lens. By feeling into the divine in you, are you able to see the divine in each of these people? One by one, imagine bowing to them, saying, "The divine in me recognizes and honors the divine in you." How does it feel to see the people in your life this way? Is it easy or hard? If it's hard, what is causing the resistance?

If you can't recognize the divine in someone, a judgment is in the way, and you know what that means. Use your Judgment-Flipping tools to figure out what these judgments are telling you about *you*. Be brutally honest. Whatever you discover, love yourself for it. Thank this person for reflecting this judgment back to you for healing. These are the small opportunities for touch-up healing that will continue to surface as long as you are human. Don't despair that they don't seem to end. Just get better and better, and swifter and swifter at healing them. *Enjoy* healing them! Every new awareness is always a cause for celebration!

Give up any vestiges of attachment you may still have to controlling or changing anyone else. You can't make anyone be nice to you, respect you, or love you. You can't make anyone give you things that you want. But in acknowledging that we're all just extensions of the same divine energetic entity, you *can* feel compassion for them . . . and the desire to change or control them will naturally fall away. The deep-sea diver wouldn't dream of making alterations to the creatures in the exotically beautiful undersea world. He appreciates them all with loving fascination.

Make a commitment, every day, to see everyone you encounter through your Namaste Lens. Look for ways to appreciate and assist people. When that becomes your foremost intention, it's difficult to ever feel slighted. If someone cuts you off on the road, and you can see that person as merely an extension of you—an extension that was in a bigger hurry than you were at the moment—and you bless that rascally road hog . . . see how much grief and stress you'll be able to spare yourself?

Honing Your Divine Communication Skills

God-Dipping is first and foremost an awareness practice—staying consistently aware of the God-presence within us all. But God-dipping also involves working out a reliable two-way communication system with that presence. How do you single out the one voice, among all those voices in your head, that represents the true you—the divine you?

The easiest way to recognize it is this: It's the voice that says it's okay; the voice that's free of fear. You know how sometimes in movies (and sometimes in real life), some seemingly horrible thing will happen, causing everything the character has worked for to fall apart, and your heart just plummets . . . but somehow within a few beats or a few syllables of dialogue, there's an energetic shift and everyone is laughing like crazy; just releasing all that tension through deep, racking belly laughs?

That's a great example of a moment when there are multiple voices to choose from, and somehow the character aligns with *this* voice—the voice of Source. The wise voice that knows that whatever just happened, it really doesn't matter. It's always the voice that feels good, but not in a shallow, momentary-gratification kind of way. It feels good in a bigger, deeper way. It's not the voice that criticizes or judges you or anyone else. It's not the voice that blames you, makes you feel guilty, or pushes you to do anything you don't feel ready to do. You must get out of your head, where all limitation is born, before you can hear the whispers of this voice.

God-Dipping means hearing what your life is saying—trusting the God-presence in you enough to tune in to its messages. You build the skill by purposefully dropping into your own higher wisdom for answers, and also by learning to recognize and honor the signs the Universe is sending you.

JuicyFeel for Connecting with the Divine You

— Go to the world of your Mirror You JuicyFeel and look deeply into your eyes reflected in that mirror.

— Find your God-self in those eyes.

— Ask your God-self any questions that come up for you.

— Remain still and quiet and see what you get.

— If it's time for you to have the answer, you may notice an image, memory, or idea surface.

— Record it in your journal, even if you're not yet sure how to interpret it. (If you didn't get anything right away, know that an answer will be coming.)

— If you feel any concerns or desires, speak them to your God-self. Do it while looking into Mirror You's eyes, unloading everything you authentically feel you need to express.

— Step away from the mirror and take a walk around your gorgeous nature setting while feeling deep appreciation for the Universe and its magnificent power. Try to access the divine certainty within you that all is exactly as it is meant to be in this moment.

— Make a cup with your hands and speak the essence of your concern, question, or desire into your cupped hands.

— Close the cup and say, "I surrender this to you, Universe. I know that you will resolve it in the manner most conducive to my highest good and the highest good of all involved. I know that if I worry about it or give it the slightest negative attention from this moment forward, I will only be impeding the speed and grace with which you are handling it for me. Thank you, as always, for your love and assistance."

— Raise your cupped hands, and with as much dramatic flair as feels appropriate to you, uncup them, releasing this concern to the Universe.

— Bask in your deep knowing that all is being handled in the best possible way. All is well.

Juicy Embodiment Practice: Send It to the Universe

Now that you've embodied the energy of confident surrender into that gesture, use your real-life cupped hands to send your concerns, questions, and desires to the Universe whenever you'd like. Watch for your answers and miracles.

Universe = God = Spirit = You

God is everywhere. God is the energy that animates each of us and connects us to all of nature, all of life, and all of one another. For me, God feels like a really close, personal friend who is always with me. I talk to God and ask God questions constantly throughout my day. Sometimes I don't hear the answers clearly, but I never, for a second, doubt that God is trying to send me the answers. I know that if I'm not getting them, it's my responsibility to find a way to turn up the volume on the connection.

As you know, I usually call God "the Universe." That just feels right to me, and reminds me that God is everywhere, all the time. I personify the Universe because it's fun for me. I like to feel that love. I choose to believe that the Universe adores and takes care of me, and that's why I get to experience it that way. If it's hard for you to personify the Universe, but easy for you to believe in Jesus or Allah or Buddha or the Law of Attraction, know that it's just a different route to the same place.

And again, if you're uncomfortable with any sort of semi-religious concept, then just think of it as your subconscious mind. You know everything. You always have and always will. When I talk about signs, or conversing with the Universe, just pretend

I'm saying to drop into your own capacity for universal knowing if that feels better to you. Just trust in *something* mysterious and wonderful. Your belief in it is what will allow it to work for you.

My favorite form of communication with the Universe is through the signs it sends me. When we get to this part about believing in signs, I know I lose some people, but I feel it's important enough for me to take that risk with you, so hear me out. Whatever you consider the cause of it to be, your brilliant subconscious is always going to nudge you to notice the things that will lead you to your highest good and greatest joy, and if you allow yourself to be led in this way, you'll get the signs you need.

Maybe it's a stretch for you to believe that people and things are strategically *placed* in your path for the sole purpose of giving you messages. If so, try on this idea: Maybe receiving signs is more a matter of allowing your all-knowing subconscious to direct your attention to specific things in your environment that will prompt you to clue in to certain messages.

Remember that at any given moment your senses are capable of detecting many, many more bits of information than your conscious mind can process. We've already seen how cleaning up our filters allows us to perceive more of the bits of information that lead us to our Juicy Joy. I believe another benefit of a clearer filter is that it allows source energy to communicate with us if we stay open to that possibility.

Unless you've been polishing your intuitive skills for a long time (we all have them), signs seldom come in as a full-on knowing. A leap of faith is almost always required. As you experience more and more confirmation, your trust in your ability to receive and interpret signs will naturally increase. In the meantime, it doesn't matter if you "believe" in signs or not. Just stay open to gleaning insights from your everyday life. A sign should feel like "Aha!" and "Yes! I knew that." It takes some practice, but paying attention to your body is a good way to start. Goosebumps, a barely discernable shiver, or any feeling of expansion and lightness in your body is a clue that the Universe is giving you confirmation.

The Universe Is Multilingual

My friend Orly reads tea leaves. My friend Deirdre talks to angels and enjoys a successful career teaching others to do the same. She has given me many uncanny, spot-on messages from my angels . . . or her angels; I'm not sure which. From my perspective, I have to believe that it's all one Source—that the energy that arranges the tea leaves in the cup for Orly is the same energy that arrives on angel wings for Dee and sends me signs from my beloved Universe.

Just like we humans can only exchange World Love, we can only connect to the divine from our human perspectives, with each of our unique imaginations providing the telephone line. Trying to get messages from angels makes me giggle. Tea leaves look like mud to me. But when I get that tingle in my gut or that chill up my spine, there's no question in my mind that I've made a right-as-rain connection. I have friends who are numerologists, card readers, pendulum swingers, pet communicators, and more than a few who talk to dead people. They're all dialing into the same energy source; they've just chosen different long-distance service providers.

You can't force signs. If you walk by a doughnut store that smells good, and you take it as a sign that you're supposed to go in and eat a doughnut, you might need some more discernment practice. It's *possible* that you're being led to go into the doughnut shop, but a true sign will feel different from a hunger pang or sugar craving. There are lots of books that give common meanings to many archetypical symbols, and while I don't like to rely heavily on them, they can be fun to have around for those times when you intuitively know you're being sent a sign but can't seem to intuit its message.

Whenever I notice a repetitive sign from an animal or some aspect of the natural world that has no immediate association for me, I look it up in one of the books by my very cool friend Dr. Steven Farmer, and I'm always blown away by the insight it affords me. My kids enjoy his books, too, and seem to get meaningful

messages from them. There are tons of books to help you understand and strengthen your intuitive abilities. Some of my favorites are by Sonia Choquette, Colette Baron-Reid, Peggy Rometo,
Denise Linn, Jeffrey Wands, and John Holland. Louise Hay's pe-
rennial classic *You Can Heal Your Life* is particularly valuable for
interpreting signs from your body.

There are unlimited languages through which the Universe
can speak with you. It's up to you to find the one that's yours. It
doesn't need to be a process of researching what's worked for other
people, though you could certainly do that if it sounds fun to you.
Most often, I believe that signs are too personal to be decoded
by anyone's system other than the one you work out for yourself
based on what feels right to you. My most meaningful messages
have all been delivered through a language that relied upon my
own personal associations, a language based on a trick I learned
over a decade ago in a dream-interpretation class.

The best way to interpret dream images is to play that old
psych game where you blurt out the very first association that
comes to you, Rorschach-test style. So if you dream about a snake,
instead of going to obvious, cliché associations or running to Dr.
Farmer's book, you say, "What does a snake mean to *me?*" Then
notice the very first association to pop up. Maybe you suddenly remember growing up with a friend who had a pet snake and being
envious because you didn't have a pet and always wanted one.
For you alone, a snake might show up in your dream to represent
something you want and perceive someone else to have.

I use this system to interpret not only my dreams (which can
be a rich source for signs in themselves), but the signs I get from
life as well. I always try to get my personal association first. If I
come up with no association, I turn to a book and see what the
symbol could represent. The symbols in books are usually based
on archetypes, meaning that even if the stated association doesn't
register in your awareness, it could still be lurking in your subconscious at the level of collective human consciousness. When
I rely on someone else's system to interpret my sign, I always feel
for whether or not the symbolism truly resonates with me. If it

doesn't, I ask the Universe for further clarification. Sometimes I'll get messages through song lyrics, movie lines or themes, or unusual memories that pop into my head.

In my case, I know that any unique motif that's repeated is a message for me. Example: Just before the dreaded day Greg and I would be telling our tweens about our divorce, my toddler niece slept at our house. Our lively before-bedtime party with her included some dancing around to Jimmy Buffett, all of us singing along at the top of our lungs to his song "Volcano."

The next morning, my young niece and I were the first ones up. We turned on the TV, and a volcano was erupting in a movie. Thinking nothing of it, I switched to her preschool channel, and we watched a cartoon where a volcano erupted, spewing grape ice cream to the delight of the characters. When that show was over, the next cartoon featured *another* volcano erupting with similar happy results.

The emotional response that bubbled up within me made it easy to intuit the message. I thanked the loving Universe for this assurance that in spite of my heavy anxiety about what was potentially about to blow for my kids, everything was going to be okay. (It was.)

It's All about Intention

Set an intention to be aware of any intuitive hits you get throughout the day, and try to write them all down in your Juicy Joy journal. It's weird but true that simply setting this intention and capturing your intuitive feelings will automatically increase your abilities. It's like you're showing the Universe that you're open and ready to value what you receive from it. The best way to prove to yourself how intuitive you are is to look back later at the impressions you recorded and note the success rate of the predictions you gleaned from them.

Often my clearest guidance pops up when I ignore an intuitive feeling that the Universe wanted me to pay attention to. Here's an example of how it sometimes plays out: I was recently in Arizona, speaking at a consciousness conference and teaching a workshop in Sedona. Other than those two events, the rest of my time there was pure play . . . eating, shopping, delving deep into craters, and climbing up spectacular red rock formations with a shaman for all kinds of sacred-land ceremonies and exciting vortex explorations.

I loved every second of the trip, but I never would have taken it if I hadn't had the "working" excuse. And on the flight home, I was thinking that there's something wrong with that, even when you love your work as much as I do. I felt an intuitive tug to blog about that insight, but after being gone for almost a week, there was so much work to catch up on that I put the idea aside, deciding I'd do it only if I "had time." My blogging (which I love to do) had become nearly nonexistent due to that "only if I have time" position where I'd been slotting it in my list of priorities.

Tackling the pileup of e-mails instead, I opened an invitation to a speaking organization. To check it out, I clicked the list of speakers. One I hadn't heard of before caught my attention, prompting me to go to his site. The first article I randomly clicked on was about the importance of play and leisure in our lives. The second one was a slap on the wrist for anyone who uses "not enough time" as an excuse for not doing all the joyful things they're drawn to do. The Universe had spoken, but if I hadn't been trained to watch for its signs, I could have easily missed the message. I immediately shut down my jam-packed inbox and opened a new blog page. I later made a valuable connection from that post.

Here's a trick I call "tarot for the woo-woo impaired." When you want an answer to a question, or a creative solution to some problem you're having, meditate and set the intention that the highest possible solution is right at your fingertips. Go to your bookshelf and pull down whichever book you're most drawn to touch. Don't think about the titles or what you know the content of the books to be. Just let your feelings guide you.

Open the book to a random page. Let your eye fall on a word, a phrase, or a sentence—whatever feels right. Read that bit of text by itself, out of context from whatever is around it, and "force associate" that text with the subject of your original inquiry. Even if no connection is immediately apparent, tell yourself you must come up with some way to link the two, and see what arises. This will often lead you to some sort of epiphany.

Another thing I do when I'm torn or indecisive about something is simply ask the Universe for clarity just before I go to sleep. While a dream will occasionally provide the answer, more often I just seem to wake up inexplicably certain about whatever issue I had been so conflicted over. I trust that some deeper understanding was stealthily woven into my consciousness while I slept, and I thank the Universe accordingly.

There's another aspect to communicating with the Universe that I don't quite understand, but since I've experienced it so many times I'll share it with you. Even when I set aside dedicated time to converse with Spirit and am sure that I have my mind crystal clear and receptive, I often don't get an answer to my question right away. But I always do get one eventually!

I don't know why the answer doesn't come when I ask. Maybe the Universe is busy, or just likes to play this game with me. But most often my questions are answered when I least expect it. When I'm involved in some tedious activity, an understanding will come to me in a flash of insight. Or I'll find my answer in signs. The trick is to simply know an answer is coming, be thankful for it in advance, and enjoy the waiting.

Watch for Signs Along the Road of Life

It's hard for the Universe to give you signs if you're holed up in a windowless room with little stimulus. Driving is one of my favorite times to watch for signs. When I'm out in my car and I don't have any particular question to pose, I just look for signs that the Universe loves me. The Universe must enjoy this because I find so much evidence! Try setting an intention to find signs every time you get in your car. It will become a habit, and the more you get used to looking for signs, the clearer they'll get. They'll be different every day, according to what you've asked or the kind of love you need that day.

You might find divine encouragement or answers to your questions on a bumper sticker, a sign in the window of a store you've never noticed before, an interesting bird, the particular twist of a tree branch. The message is almost always contained in the feeling that the thing inspires in you, or the association that pops up in your head. Notice successions in particular. Seeing multiple versions of the same message will get you over your skepticism. Ask for repetition if you're not sure about a particular sign.

It's fine to pose direct questions to the Universe, but the key is not to stretch beyond what you can believe. When you ask a question, let the Universe decide how to answer it. Don't say: "If I'm meant to marry her, Universe, show me a white Lexus right now with a license plate that starts with her initials." If you choose to put that out there but don't see the Lexus, you need to consider the possibility that you already knew the answer you were looking for.

A better result would come from an open inquiry, such as, "Universe, show me something to help me get clarity about this commitment I'm considering." Then, without trying too hard, see what you notice next. Pay attention to your body for how to interpret the signs. If you pass a sculpture that resembles a tiered wedding cake, and your gut uncomfortably clenches, trust that the Universe has spoken. If the same sculpture inspires an excited little flutter in your heart, rejoice in that positive confirmation. Your uncertainty might simply have been fear caused by a limiting belief.

It may seem like you're imagining signs and their messages. Duh. Of course you are—your imagination is the language the Universe uses to communicate with you. That doesn't make the process any less real. Even if you think you might be manipulating the signs you interpret, so what? If they help you, don't worry about that.

I had a driving epiphany a few years ago in a rental car on my way to spread Juicy Joy to 1,500 Missourians. Lost in thought about the presentation I was about to give, I suddenly became aware that the desolate, rural road I was traveling was chock-full of unnecessary stop signs. It felt kind of *Twilight Zone*–ish to keep stopping when there was never anyone coming on the cross streets. The *Twilight Zone*–ish sensation was my cue that the Universe wanted my attention.

I immediately clued into the message that I needed to make a point to stop and center myself more frequently. Since that day, I've been inspired to make every stop sign I see a message to me. It's helped me curb my tendency to ruminate, plan, and spend way too much time in my head. Now every time I come to a stop sign or a red light, I use it as a cue to also *mentally* stop and assess: *Am I in head-space right now or present-moment heart-space? Am I giving attention to what I want or what I don't want?* Then I adjust. You could argue that I made that up for myself and it's not a real sign from the Universe, but it doesn't matter. The practice serves me, either way.

Since I tend to overschedule and rush from place to place, I've also made a conscious habit of being grateful for delays. I choose to view any point in my day when I unexpectedly have to wait for something—long lines, traffic, late friends, appointment delays—as gifts from a benevolent Universe that wants me to slow down. I give thanks for these moments, recognizing that they're opportunities for me to take a break from my busy mind and fill up on God Love. (And of course, since I've stopped resisting these incidents, I almost never encounter them anymore.)

One of my more spectacular moments of drive-time sign reading took place when I connected with the energy of my pregnant sister's not-yet-born baby. For weeks I'd been talking to the baby in spirit, letting it know how excited we all were to meet it and what a great choice it had made in parents. My sister and her husband did not want to know the baby's sex, but I'd been having strong intuitive feelings that it was a girl.

My sister called me as I was driving that day to tell me that a careless sonogram technician had just leaked information that pointed clearly to the fact that the baby was a boy. I felt a gut sense that the information was wrong, but for the moment, kept it to myself. When we hung up, I dialed in telepathically to my future sweet niece, and asked her to please show me a sign that I was correct in my hunch about her gender.

Within seconds, I drove past a huge pile of pale pink pipe stacked along the side of the road, presumably for some imminent pipe-laying project. Even though I had asked for the sign, I got a bit tingly from that enormous pile of pinkness. In awe, I asked her for a second sign, and immediately a pink car showed up in my rearview mirror. Thrilled by the speed and clarity of her responses, I boldly requested a third sign. As the pink VW Beetle passed me, I spotted a fluffy pink teddy bear in the rear window. Major chills of confirmation. I immediately reported my prediction to my sister, and I've felt a special bond with my precious *niece* ever since.

I often get questions about signs that require other people's involvement, like the driver of the pink car being exactly where I needed her to be that day. You could assume it's random coincidence or simply a matter of my filter allowing me to notice the pink car. Or you could open your mind to the possibility that there's more to it than that.

It's fascinating and mind-boggling, and I don't pretend to understand all of its intricacies, but there is a metaphysical principle known as "the infinite organizing power of the Universe" that says that people come into other people's lives with just the right messages and learning opportunities at just the right time—while, simultaneously, *those* people are being given the signs and lessons they need as well.

In a way, the judgment we sometimes make about someone thinking that he or she is "the center of the universe" is not so far off, nor is it cause for judgment. In a very real metaphysical sense, you *are* the center of your universe, just as everyone you interact with is the center of theirs. The Universe's infinite organizing power is not meant to be understood by our human brains. Our job is just to accept, trust, and appreciate it.

Dig for Gold in Your Signs

The whole business of interpreting signs can become remarkably complex and rewarding if you allow it to be. I've come to realize that there's often a deeper level I can get to when I put time and effort into decoding a sign. I've started to gauge the level to which a recognized sign tugs at me as an indication of how much introspection I should give to it.

Flying back from giving Juicy Joy presentations in New York recently, I met a man on a plane. I often make friends on planes, but this one was different in that he felt intriguingly familiar to me. Since there was something about him that tugged at my attention, I knew that he had been delivered to me by the Universe, but I couldn't get a clear read on the message. We chatted, shared a brief layover where he sweetly surprised me with sushi to take on my next flight, and that was that. Alone on the next leg of my journey, I went into a meditation to ask Universe about the sign. Right away, I got a name: "Bernard Mickey Wrangle."

The guy had told me his name, and that wasn't it. Yet the name Bernard Mickey Wrangle was familiar. Then I remembered—it was the name of a character in *Still Life with Woodpecker,* a Tom Robbins novel I had read and loved more than 20 years ago. The character had red hair, and so did my plane friend, so I rolled my eyes and said, "Seriously, Universe? Just because of the red hair?" The Universe laughed (we have that kind of relationship) and pointed out that I'd encountered dozens of redheaded men since reading that book, and none before had ever made me think of Bernard Mickey Wrangle.

So I went to my gut-association trick. Who was Bernard Mickey Wrangle to me? He was a philosopher, a romantic, a social activist with a sense of humor—a smart, gutsy, world-changing rebel with the soul of a poet. I hadn't talked nearly enough with my plane friend to know much about him, but I could see how his energy in some ways matched the energy I attributed to the character of Bernard (aka "the Woodpecker"). Because I was attracted to the plane guy's energy, much of the association may have been projection, but that's irrelevant to the task of figuring out the meanings of signs. The Universe had used him to give me the name Bernard Mickey Wrangle, so that's what I needed to focus on.

If everything I encounter is a mirror (and it is), what was the Woodpecker mirroring for me? I acknowledged that I was fancying myself a bit of a philosopher and social reformer, and Bernard had definitely been a model of authenticity. He was also an unapologetic, voraciously lusty character, which had made him thrilling to read about. He had juice.

But none of that felt like a message I could learn from, so I asked, "Universe, what do I need to know about this?" Only then did I remember the question Tom Robbins posed at the beginning and end of that novel: "How do you make love stay?" The quick flush in my face was the "bingo!" from the Universe. I suddenly recognized that I was still wearing a dull, fuzzy, juice-robbing cloak of guilt over not having been able to "make love stay" in my marriage to Greg. I hadn't realized the depth of my subconscious self-incrimination until that moment.

I immediately downloaded *Still Life with Woodpecker* to my Kindle and reread it to find out what conclusion Bernard Mickey Wrangle had come to on this all-important question. In typical Robbins fashion, the question was left provokingly yet satisfactorily *un*answered. My revisit to the deliciously subversive world of that counterculture classic comforted and enlightened me. If Robbins —whom I consider a genius on matters of the human condition— didn't know how to make love stay, then I could certainly stop beating myself up for not being able to figure it out either.

And who decided that romantic love is always *meant* to stay, anyway? If you accept the worthwhile premise that love is the main event—the reason we're here—then it seems to me that the most important goal should be simply to love in this moment. And the next moment. And the next. If the love we feel for one particular person changes form along the way, why should that be deemed a failure? We make it a failure with our beliefs—the ones imposed on us by our society—and hadn't I rewritten those laws for myself? I finally felt the surreptitious cloak of residual guilt sliding away.

To recap: I met a guy on a plane. I recognized it as a sign, and I made the conscious choice to explore it until it delivered something exquisitely meaningful and liberating for me. You can do this even if you think the whole idea of signs from the Universe is bullshit. Taking time for genuine self-inquiry and introspection *with the expectation that something valuable will come of it* will always lead your subconscious to reveal something useful to you. Allowing yourself to be intuitively guided by triggers in your outer world just streamlines the process.

Since the intuitive tug about my plane friend felt substantial to me, I took the time for a meditative inquiry with the Universe, which revealed the deeper message I needed to hear. But I could have more casually interpreted the encounter in a number of equally valid, less profound ways. For example, I also acknowledged that it was a sign that interesting single men were abundantly available and could pop into my life at any moment. That interpretation was just as valid, and since I had just begun giving myself permission to consider dating, I accepted it as an additional message from the Universe. I knew that strengthening *that* belief in my filter would serve me well.

If I had a different filter, one clouded with lousy, ill-serving beliefs, I might have subconsciously interpreted the encounter as proof that men I'm attracted to are always going to be unavailable —geographically or otherwise. Can you see how someone who had not worked on cleaning up her filter might draw that unhappy conclusion, thereby reinforcing the limiting belief? And in reinforcing that crappy belief, she'd be ensuring that it was her reality.

Make Arrangements with the Universe

The Universe and I have an agreement. Since I'm still learning to fully step into my ever-evolving intuitive abilities, I've asked it to not only give me signs, but to *give me signs in triplicate* when I'm being particularly thick in receiving its communications.

We developed this system because unless I've specifically asked a question, I'm often clueless about signs, especially the first time they're sent.

Usually, when something unique makes a second appearance in my life within a short time, that's when it occurs to me to wonder if it's a sign. And since we have this prior agreement going, I'll say, "Okay, Universe. You know the drill. If this is a message from you, I'm going to need it one more time." The Universe has been wonderfully patient to indulge me with this arrangement, and at the appearance of the third sign, I always show my gratitude and faith by taking some kind of action around that message, whatever I most intuitively interpret it to be.

Here's an example: Just before I sent my Juicy Joy proposal to Hay House, I was giving a local workshop and a woman made a joke about me that referenced the oft-quoted diner-scene line from the movie *When Harry Met Sally*. I was apparently a bit zealous in my delivery—which happened to be taking place at a café where the attendees were encouraged to snack and drink during the workshop—and this woman told the waiter, "I'll have what she's having." We all laughed, and I thought nothing more about it.

Less than a week later, at a Bert Oliva motivational seminar with my son, the man sitting next to me noticed the way I was dancing and made the exact same joke about me by quoting that same movie line to those sharing our row. Hmm. Kind of weird for that to come up twice. So I had my sign-number-two conversation with the Universe, and left it at that.

It was just three days later, at a meditation and yoga gathering with some of my closest girlfriends, that one of them was prompted by my excitability over a story I was sharing, to use that *exact same movie line* about me. I felt the momentary silencing of the world—the quick chill up my spine that often accompanies the third sign. But I had no idea how to interpret this one, so I laid the conundrum out for my friends.

One of them—known to be highly intuitive—said, "It reminds me of that Tolstoy thing you do in your creativity workshop. I bet the sign is about you sending your proposal off to Hay House this week."

In my *Juicy Joy for Creativity* workshop, I reference Leo Tolstoy's famous and controversial essay, "What Is Art?" in which he makes the assertion that "art is infection." He means that when the artist is moved to create, he feels something so intensely that he is, in effect, afflicted by the thing he must express. And then the audience of that art, upon being exposed to it, is immediately infected by the contagious energy the artist has imprinted onto his creation.

I decided to accept that interpretation of my sign from the Universe. I decided to believe that "I'll have what she's having," was an indication that the world was craving a widespread infection of Juicy Joy. Satisfying that craving became my not-so-humble intention for this book.

God-Dipping in a Juicy Nutshell

God-Dipping is the ability to stay consistently aware of the divine tapestry that connects you and me and every single thing we experience. It's learning to devise a reliable communication system with the Universe—or however you choose to term source energy—so that you can dip into that inexhaustible resource whenever you'd like.

We've been trained to see ourselves as separate from one another and from divine energy, but that is such a false premise! Feeling your rich, juicy connection to everyone and everything is as simple as opening your heart and *deciding* to feel it. It feels fantastic!

Understanding your connection to others and showing your appreciation for them uplifts you as much as it uplifts those you bestow your blessings upon. People can feel when you are truly appreciating them, even if they don't acknowledge it. Your appreciation vibration will allow them—and *you*—to flourish. Tapping into and feeding the ever-present energy that binds us all together makes everything else fall into place. You're a better parent, friend,

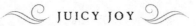

and spouse; you're healthier and more energetic. Research continually shows that when we help others, we feel better ourselves.

All the steps you've taken toward your Juicy Joy have led you to this ultimate God-Dipping practice. Life loves you. It always has, and it always will. Your determination to receive that love and unconditionally *love life back* will forever seal your Juicy-Joyful fate.

GO FORTH IN JUICY, JUICY JOY!

You can now confidently claim, "I've earned an advanced degree from the University of Me." You know how spectacularly powerful your feelings are, and you have a toolbox chock-full of simple, juicy ways to create the feelings you want for yourself. You know how to access the flow of love that's always available to you, from God and from the world. You've had hardships, which have taught you valuable things about your beliefs and what you want. You've done the difficult self-examination work of clearing your filter of any influences that aren't serving your greatest good and your yummiest joy. You've gotten real with yourself about your deepest desires—and you know you deserve to have them.

If you've stayed true to the processes along your Juicy Joy journey, you've undoubtedly shifted some significant core beliefs and are seeing ample, scrumptious evidence of that in your life circumstances. But our filters are tricky companions, so you can never let your guard down. Juicy Joy is a way of life, and you must continue its diligent practice forever. Since Juicy Joy feels so good and brings so many rewards, this shouldn't be a difficult commitment to make. It becomes simply a matter of staying awake to your life, to your power, and having an unswerving dedication to living your juice.

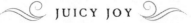

Are You Wanting Correctly?

To make sure you continue seeing that scrumptious evidence, let's do a quick checkup on your current desires to see if you are *wanting* correctly.

NakedWriting: Current Wants

- Draw a vertical line down the center of a new page in your journal.

- On the left side, write a few of your current top desires.

- On the right side, listening to your body and not your head, jot down the top few honest *feelings* you have about each of these desires.

Done? Okay, look at the feeling words. Are any of them negative? If they are, it means that you're focused on the *lack* of what you want. You can't get it that way. You can't pull these desires into your life until you start authentically having nothing but positive feelings about them (which will indicate you believe they can be yours.)

Wanting should always feel delicious. If it doesn't, that's your cue to apply your Juicy Joy tools until it does. Judgment-Flip your doubts away. Fill a taco and spend some generous time luxuriating in a JuicyFeel about it. Wiggle your hips when you say "I want." Say it with a gleam in your eye. Until you can want this way, there's no point in wanting at all.

NakedWriting: Revisit Your Juicy Joy Pizza

Remember the pizza you drew when you first embarked on your Juicy Joy journey? Let's do that again.

- Draw a circle the size of a small plate and divide it, like a pizza, into eight slices.

- Break down your life into eight different categories, however that makes sense for you. The categories might be the same ones you chose for your last pizza, or a few might be different now. Label each slice.

- Look at one pizza slice and observe your immediate feeling when you consider that area of your life. Simply feel it; don't think about it. If you start making a mental list of pros and cons, you're thinking, not feeling.

- Give that slice a rating, from one to ten, to describe how much joy you're feeling in that area of your life, ten being the highest amount of joy.

- Rate the rest of the slices.

- Did you bump up your scores? Do you feel you have the tools to continue bumping them up, even as the categories change over time?

Juicy Joy students who have been diligent in their practices always have enormously juicier pizzas to report. If you found an area of your life that did not get a high score, can you now recognize the possible reasons for that? Are there judgments you're not willing to look at and balance? What are your payoffs? Are you still prioritizing security, approval, respect, or some kind of outer-originated stroke? How can you *give yourself* the payoff you seek, so that you can take responsibility for creating your Juicy Joy?

Remember that taking responsibility just means knowing what you want, and accessing the feelings of already having it. It's not your responsibility to figure out how it will happen, and the more you concern yourself with the *how*, the more you may be getting in your own way.

Are You Open to Receive?

Are you convinced yet that the Universe adores you and constantly orchestrates on your behalf? If not, you may be in a vibration of *dis*allowing, which will keep your Juicy Joy Reality Plan perpetually out of reach. More time with your JuicyFeels will turn the vibration around. It could be that you're looking for solid evidence too soon and giving your attention to the lack of it, instead of keeping yourself immersed in the feelings of what you want, with the full expectation that it will come to you.

I know this is a tough one. When you really, really want something—and believe that you're putting all the right energy into your JuicyFeels and trying to live in a joyful state of anticipation—it sucks when the thing you want doesn't show up. There are three possibilities that explain why this might happen, and all are in the interest of your highest good. One possibility is that you just need to wait a bit longer for the thing you want in order for it to give you the feelings you believe it will give you. Sometimes you simply can't see that from your limited human perspective. It's entirely probable that the thing you want is coming—just not in the time frame you've requested.

The second possibility is that you're wanting release from an experience that holds a critical learning opportunity for you—one that you've yet to recognize and grow from. Or maybe you have recognized it and grown to a degree, but need to go even deeper and grow further in order for this experience to yield spectacular results.

Remember how our greatest suffering can be a prerequisite for our greatest bliss? You may need to experience contrast right now so that your most perfect dream can be born from it; or you may be stuck in a repetitive story cycle that has a profoundly transformational message for you to absorb before you can move on. You must strive to find the message while implicitly trusting that the Universe knows what it's doing.

The last possibility is sometimes the hardest to consider. What if the thing you want simply will not bring you the feelings you think it will? That is often also difficult to know from your limited perspective. How many times have you pined away for a particular guy or woman (one you've endowed with all sorts of imaginary qualities) and then later found out that he or she was not

the person you imagined at all? See? The Universe does love and protect you, and sometimes it's protecting you from yourself.

It all comes down to feelings. All the things you think you want—you wouldn't want them if they didn't hold a promise for a certain feeling. If you've been putting out a desire that hasn't yet shown up, let's see if we can get some clarity on that now.

NakedWriting: As-of-Yet Unfulfilled Desires

- Again, draw a vertical line down the center of a page in your journal and write your current desires in the left column.

- This time, drop down into your gut and isolate the feelings you believe each item on your list will *bring you* and write those feelings in the right column. You should be pretty good at this sort of thing by now. Any item could have several feelings associated with it.

- In comparing the two lists, can you recognize that the feelings are what you're really after?

If there's a particular job you want to have, why do you want it? Maybe financial freedom, maybe security, maybe fun and adventure, the chance to meet like-minded people, the chance to learn something you've always wanted to learn. Now imagine, just for a moment, that the Universe—the one that loves you madly and unconditionally and always wants what's best for you—is privy to a much more inclusive understanding of this particular job, and it knows that the position will positively not bring you those feelings you're attributing to it.

As hard as you try to get this job, the Universe might be making sure you don't get it, while at the same time it might be sending you multiple clear, in-your-face signs about another job—one that *would* bring you all those feelings you want. If you sit around pissed off at the Universe for not getting you that first job you were trying so hard to manifest, you'll miss all the signs about the better situation.

Look at your list again. Go to alpha state and ask the Universe if any of the things you have listed are *not* a true match to the feelings you expect them to generate. If you get any immediate impressions, write them in your journal. If not, be on the lookout for signs and other gifts from the Universe. Promise the Universe that you'll be open to receiving them.

I remember once feeling super pressed for time and asking the Universe for help with that. I had ridiculous to-do lists on top of my writing obligations, and to compound the matter, I developed insomnia. My first instinct was a sarcastic "Oh, perfect. Sleep deprivation is just what I need right now." But I knew that resistance would only make the insomnia worse, so I got myself into the feeling place of authentically thanking the Universe for my sleeplessness, trusting against all reason that it was a gift somehow.

I'd get writing ideas while lying awake, so I started getting up to write. One day it finally occurred to me that I wasn't ever tired. I was feeling energetic and clear on just an average of three hours of sleep a night. The insomnia was my answered prayer! I had asked God for extra hours, and God had said, "Okay, how about four extra hours a day? Is that good?" And I had almost missed this generous gift by knocking myself out with some kind of sleep aid! When I got caught up with the things I needed to do, the insomnia vanished.

Focus on the feelings on the right side of your list. Doesn't it make you feel juicier to read this column than the column on the left? Consider the idea of restuffing your taco—this time only stuffing it with the *feelings* you want, not the specific ways you imagine getting them. If that idea feels okay to you, give it a try. This is the essence of surrender, and the Universe will find it irresistible. You will be dazzled by its compliance.

Stay Juicy, My Love

One of my favorite teachers of Buddhism told me: "There is no such thing as an enlightened being. There are only enlightened moments." You're never done. There's never going to be a morning when you wake up and say, "Enlightenment—check!" Even popular modern-day masters who are known for having profound epiphanies that mark significant shifts in their lives will tell you that the big moment was just one among many that happened to stand out more prominently for them. For most of us, our enlightenment comes crumb by crumb . . . with an exhilarating little spurt here and there. Know that you are perfect in your imperfection, and be kind and gentle with yourself.

Be giddy-happy about your understanding that everyone is a mirror for you and the people who show up in your life are there to show you how you feel about yourself. What a handy trick! Instead of striving in vain to get your needs met by others, you are now in the driver's seat! If you want respect from a boss, learn how to respect yourself. If you want passionate love from a partner, start loving yourself with passionate adoration. Your energy is their energy is everyone's energy, and you have the power to create whatever you want!

Since we're all energetically intertwined, loving yourself and disarming your self-judgments benefits everyone else, too. There's a Buddhist principle that says we all would love one another fully and completely if we were free of our limitations and masks. The enemy is never another person—the enemy is always unconsciousness. When we awaken consciousness in ourselves, we contribute immeasurably to the awakening of the world.

Say "I love you" silently in your head every time you interact with anyone. The busy barista at your favorite coffee shop. Your snooty hairdresser. Your meanest neighbor. Your cranky dry cleaner. "I see the divine in you." "I love you." "I feel the human connection between us right now." You'll be blown away by the magic that simple practice will create in your life.

Are you accepting and enthusiastically embracing the full truth of where you are *right now?* Have you decided, definitively, that everything in your life has been absolutely as it was meant to be to bring you to this precise place? You get to choose your belief in this moment and in every future moment that you're alive, so choose to see each moment as perfect!

If there's something that comes up in any of those moments that you feel yourself having a negative feeling about, welcome the feeling and use your Judgment-Flipping skills to figure out what message the loving Universe is sending you. Learn from it, thank it, and rejoice, knowing that every time you do that you're releasing the need to ever experience that particular type of unwanted circumstance again.

Now that these skills are becoming second nature to you, every moment truly *is* a perfect moment! How could it be otherwise? We can only move forward, but you've discovered that loving the hell out of this precise moment, exactly as it is, is the key to moving forward toward the kinds of experiences you most desire. Love and inspiration are all around you, all the time! The Universe wants you to succeed and be happy. Living your unique, personal flavor of Juicy Joy is your highest calling! It's so easy to love any moment, no matter what it brings, when you passionately love the company you're keeping in that moment—which will always, without exception, be . . . glorious, gutsy, divine *you*.

GUIDE TO FANTASTIC
RESOURCES

Although many of my most metaphysically savvy friends have told me that they've gotten tremendous benefit from *Juicy Joy*, I wrote it with the intention of bringing over new recruits to the ever-burgeoning world of spiritual and metaphysical personal development. I was accordingly selective in my use of quotes, being careful not to overutilize established woo-woo icons, and instead choosing wisdom from more mainstream-embraced geniuses like Albert Einstein, Oprah Winfrey, and assorted literary figures.

This resource guide is where I give my woo-woo heroes their due. Assuming you've crossed over the bridge and are ready to immerse yourself in the deliciously real world of spiritual New Thought, following are some alphabetical lists of programs, resources, teachers, and authors I wholeheartedly recommend. Many of them are regular guests on live webinars in my Juicy Joy online trainings, so if you'd like the opportunity to interact with them personally, check the Juicy Joy online community for details.

Since I am continually evolving in my pursuit of ever-wider realms of authenticity and self-love, I will forever be posting powerful new ways for you to access your Juicy Joy at the online community. I look forward to meeting you at **JuicyJoy.com**, where

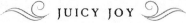

you will also find links and up-to-date information for all of the following resources. I've made a silly attempt to group them for you, though most overlap into several categories.

My Favorite Authors with Fascinating, Powerful Messages (Many of Whom Also Offer Trainings)

Joan Borysenko, www.joanborysenko.com
Gregg Braden, www.greggbraden.com
Richard Carlson, www.richardcarlson.com
Alan Cohen, www.alancohen.com
Stephen R. Covey, www.stephencovey.com
David Deida, www.deida.info
Mike Dooley, www.tut.com/about/mikedooley
Oriah Mountain Dreamer, www.oriahmountaindreamer.com
Wayne Dyer, www.drwaynedyer.com
Arielle Ford, www.arielleford.com
Debbie Ford, www.debbieford.com
Elizabeth Gilbert, www.elizabethgilbert.com
Daniel Goleman, www.danielgoleman.info
Don Joseph Goewey, www.donjosephgoewey.com
Jean Haner, www.wisdomofyourface.com
Gay and Kathlyn Hendricks, www.hendricks.com
Robert Holden, www.happiness.co.uk
Byron Katie, www.thework.com
Elizabeth Lesser, www.elizabethlesser.net
Bruce Lipton, www.brucelipton.com
Summer McStravick, www.flowdreaming.com
Dan Millman, www.peacefulwarrior.com
Gretchen Rubin, www.gretchenrubin.com
don Miguel Ruiz, www.miguelruiz.com
Daylle Deanna Schwartz, www.daylle.com
Martin Seligman, www.authentichappiness.sas.upenn.edu
Eldon Taylor, www.eldontaylor.com
Regena Thomashauer, www.mamagenas.com
Eckhart Tolle, www.eckharttolle.com

Joe Vitale, **www.mrfire.com**
Neale Donald Walsch, **www.nealedonaldwalsch.com**

My Favorite Trainings Not
Connected to Particular Authors

The Hero's Journey, recovery workship for codependency, **www.codependency-recovery.com**
The Living Course, **www.pdcseminars.com**
Omega Institute, holistic studies in Rhinebeck, NY, **www .zeomega.com**
The Sedona Method (David Ellzey), **www.davidellzey.com**
Self Discovery Life Mastery, **www.selfdiscoverytechniques.com**
The Silva Method, **www.silvamethod.com**
Transcendental Meditation, **www.tm.org**

My Favorite Phenomenal Coaches and Wisdom
Spreaders (Many of Whom Are Also Authors)

Jack Canfield, **www.jackcanfield.com**
Ernest Chu, **www.soulcurrency.org**
Rachael Jayne Groover, **www.theyinproject.com**
Brad Lamm, **www.bradlamm.com**
Michele Landers, **www.michelelanders.com**
Lilou Macé, **www.liloumace.com**
Robert Mack, **www.happinessfromtheinsideout.com**
Dawn Maslar, **www.dawnmaslar.com**
Karen McCrocklin, **www.karenmccrocklin.com**
Christian Pankhurst, **www.christianpankhurst.com**
Ricky Powell, **www.lifelonghappiness.com**
Cheryl Richardson, **www.cherylrichardson.com**
Anthony Robbins, **www.tonyrobbins.com**
Jill Rogers, **www.thesevensacredsteps.com**
Ram Giri, **www.skillsforawakening.com**
Marci Shimoff, **www.happyfornoreason.com**
Tej Steiner, **www.tejsteiner.com**

My Favorite Mind-Body-Spirit Integrators (Who Are Also Authors and Trainers)

Deepak Chopra, **www.deepakchopra.com**
Louise Hay, **www.louisehay.com**
Christiane Northrup, **www.drnorthrup.com**
Caroline Sutherland, **www.carolinesutherland.com**
Marianne Williamson, **www.marianne.com**

My Favorite Intuitives and Energy Workers (Many of Whom Are Also Authors or Trainers)

Abraham/Jerry & Esther Hicks, **www.abraham-hicks.com**
Deirdre Abrami, **www.thehealingcenteronline.com**
Colette Baron-Reid, **www.colettebaronreid.com**
Sonia Choquette, **www.soniachoquette.com**
Jill Dahne, **www.jilldahne.com**
Steven Farmer, **www.drstevenfarmer.com**
Shakti Gawain, **www.shaktigawain.com**
Roger Hanson, **www.spiritinspiredlife.com**
John Holland, **www.johnholland.com**
Sunny Dawn Johnston, **www.sunnydawnjohnston.com**
Deborah King, **www.deborahkingcenter.com**
Denise Linn, **www.deniselinn.com**
Barb Powell, **www.barb-powell.com**
Peggy Rometo, **www.peggyrometo.com**
Rachael Schmidt, **www.rachaelschmidt.com**
Deb Snyder, **www.heartglowparenting.com**
Sandra Anne Taylor, **www.sandrataylor.net**
Asia Voight, **www.asiavoight.com**
Jeffrey Wands, **www.jeffreywands.com**
Brian Weiss, **www.brianweiss.com**
Darren Weissman, **www.drdarrenweissman.com**
Michelle Whitedove, **www.michellewhitedove.com**

My Favorite Sources of Time-Tested Wisdom

The Bhagavad-Gita, **www.bhagavad-gita.org**

Buddhism (see especially Pema Chödrön and Thich Nhat Hanh), **www.plumvillage.org**

Joseph Campbell, **www.jcf.org**

Albert Einstein

Franz Kafka

Carl Jung, **www.cgjungpage.org**

Osho, **www.osho.com**

The Tao te Ching (I like Stephen Mitchell's translation), **www .stephenmitchellbooks.com**

~C~

ACKNOWLEDGMENTS

From the juiciest corners of my heart, I thank all of the teachers listed in the preceding resource guide. They are my heroes, models, and masters. They have shaped me in all the ways I'm most proud of having been shaped. Likewise, I thank every member of my family of origin for every experience and opportunity that led me to evolve into the glorious, gutsy self I have become.

I owe a vast debt of gratitude to my remarkable children, Tucker and Lily Kate—as well as their father, Greg—for inspiring me and granting me the time and space to follow my passion for synthesizing and spreading this information. I am blessed beyond measure to share my journey with each of them.

I thank all the students of my Juicy Joy trainings and those who attend my presentations, both near and far, for their curiosity, open minds, and ready hearts. It was your enthusiasm and generous feedback that gave me the confidence to consolidate the Juicy Joy principles into this format.

For understanding me and loving me in ways no other possibly could, I thank my remarkable siblings, Aimee and Michael. I adore you both to the ends of the earth. Buckets of gratitude and love are also extended to Sarah Lester and everyone in my Emerald Pointe tribe, to my "royal secret sisterhood," and to my beloved community of like-minded friends and lightworkers. Each of you owns prime real estate in my heart.

Wild applause goes to the amazingly talented Kim Weiss for the Juicy Joy song! And of course, enormous gratitude to Louise Hay, Reid Tracy, Shannon Littrell, Christy Salinas, Donna Abate, and all of the divine beings at Hay House—not only for your trust in me, but for all you've done and continue to do to spread consciousness and the wisdom of love to every crevice of this world.

ABOUT THE AUTHOR

Lisa McCourt has always been passionate about . . . *passion.* Her quirky addiction to personal growth, love, and un-suppressible joy has fueled a prolific writing, speaking, and teaching career that has touched the lives of millions. In just over a decade, Lisa has published more than three dozen books that have been translated into 11 languages, been featured on CNN and PBS, won seven publishing awards, and sold more than five and a half million copies.

Lisa's dedication to teaching the combined arts of radical authenticity and unwavering self-adoration evolved from her earlier focus on writing parenting books and children's books that helped kids grow up feeling unconditionally lovable and valuable. A frank and dynamic speaker, she has taught her Juicy-Joyful, sometimes shocking, always transformative methods to thousands in her popular presentations and online trainings. Lisa lives in sunny South Florida, where she shares her ever-evolving personal-growth pursuits with her two self-loving kids. Visit her at **www.LisaMcCourt.com.**

NOTES

 NOTES

NOTES

NOTES

NOTES

NOTES

NOTES

NOTES

Hay House Titles of Related Interest

YOU CAN HEAL YOUR LIFE, the movie, starring Louise L. Hay & Friends
(available as a 1-DVD program and an expanded 2-DVD set)
Watch the trailer at: **www.LouiseHayMovie.com**

THE SHIFT, the movie,
starring Dr. Wayne W. Dyer
(available as a 1-DVD program and an expanded 2-DVD set)
Watch the trailer *at:* **www.DyerMovie.com**

~

ENOUGH ALREADY: The Power of Radical Contentment,
by Alan Cohen

THE LAW OF ATTRACTION: The Basics of the Teachings of Abraham ®,
by Esther and Jerry Hicks

QUEST: A Guide for Creating Your Own Vision Quest,
by Denise Linn and Meadow Linn (available August 2012)

WHO WOULD YOU BE WITHOUT YOUR STORY?:
Dialogues with Byron Katie, edited by Carol Williams

YOU CAN CREATE AN EXCEPTIONAL LIFE,
by Louise Hay & Cheryl Richardson

All of the above are available at your local bookstore,
or may be ordered by contacting Hay House (see next page).

~

We hope you enjoyed this Hay House book. If you'd like to receive our online catalog featuring additional information on Hay House books and products, or if you'd like to find out more about the Hay Foundation, please contact:

Hay House, Inc., P.O. Box 5100, Carlsbad, CA 92018-5100
(760) 431-7695 or (800) 654-5126
(760) 431-6948 (fax) or (800) 650-5115 (fax)
www.hayhouse.com® • **www.hayfoundation.org**

Published and distributed in Australia by:
Hay House Australia Pty. Ltd., 18/36 Ralph St., Alexandria NSW 2015 •
Phone: 612-9669-4299 • *Fax:* 612-9669-4144 • www.hayhouse.com.au

Published and distributed in the United Kingdom by:
Hay House UK, Ltd., 292B Kensal Rd., London W10 5BE • *Phone:*
44-20-8962-1230 • *Fax:* 44-20-8962-1239 • www.hayhouse.co.uk

Published and distributed in the Republic of South Africa by:
Hay House SA (Pty), Ltd., P.O. Box 990, Witkoppen 2068 •
Phone/Fax: 27-11-467-8904 • www.hayhouse.co.za

Published in India by: Hay House Publishers India,
Muskaan Complex, Plot No. 3, B-2, Vasant Kunj, New Delhi 110 070 •
Phone: 91-11-4176-1620 • *Fax:* 91-11-4176-1630 • www.hayhouse.co.in

Distributed in Canada by: Raincoast,
9050 Shaughnessy St., Vancouver, B.C. V6P 6E5 • *Phone:*
(604) 323-7100 • *Fax:* (604) 323-2600 • www.raincoast.com

Take Your Soul on a Vacation

Visit **www.HealYourLife.com®** to regroup, recharge, and reconnect with your own magnificence. Featuring blogs, mind-body-spirit news, and life-changing wisdom from Louise Hay and friends.

Visit **www.HealYourLife.com** today!

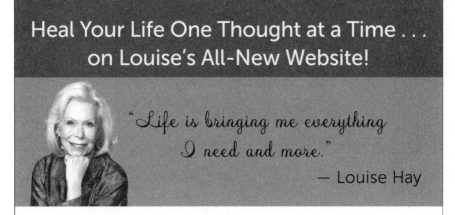